SELF-LOVE
Journey

SELF-LOVE Journey

MELISSA FOREMAN, BSHCM

Copyright © 2024 Melissa Foreman, BSHCM. All rights reserved.

No part of this publication may be reproduced, stored in a retrieval system or transmitted in any form or by any means, electronic, mechanical, photocopying, recording or otherwise, without prior permission of Halo Publishing International.

The views and opinions expressed in this book are those of the author and do not necessarily reflect the official policy or position of Halo Publishing International. Any content provided by our authors are of their opinion and are not intended to malign any religion, ethnic group, club, organization, company, individual or anyone or anything.

For permission requests, write to the publisher, addressed "Attention: Permissions Coordinator," at the address below.

Halo Publishing International
7550 W IH-10 #800, PMB 2069,
San Antonio, TX 78229

First Edition, November 2024
ISBN: 978-1-63765-696-9
Library of Congress Control Number: 2024921461

The information contained within this book is strictly for informational purposes. Unless otherwise indicated, all the names, characters, businesses, places, events and incidents in this book are either the product of the author's imagination or used in a fictitious manner. Any resemblance to actual persons, living or dead, or actual events is purely coincidental.

Halo Publishing International is a self-publishing company that publishes adult fiction and non-fiction, children's literature, self-help, spiritual, and faith-based books. We continually strive to help authors reach their publishing goals and provide many different services that help them do so. We do not publish books that are deemed to be politically, religiously, or socially disrespectful, or books that are sexually provocative, including erotica. Halo reserves the right to refuse publication of any manuscript if it is deemed not to be in line with our principles. Do you have a book idea you would like us to consider publishing? Please visit www.halopublishing.com for more information.

Self-Love Journey

I attend to my needs by listening to my heart. My inner essence guides me to know what's best. I respect my limits. I answer the requests of my body and soul. I learn to love myself. It is a blessing in disguise when you are asked not prejudge your current set of circumstances.

If you do not show forgiveness to others, no one else will show it to you. Archangel Michael, I asked you and the most high God to protect me and my family with your powerful shell. Surround us with your powerful shield, and surround us with your purple light, which allows only pure love to penetrate and stay with me day and night and keep me and my loved ones safe.

Love you

As above, so below.

Contents

Prologue	15
Self-Love Journey	17
Be the Change	18
Step One	24
Daily Prayers of Protection	25
"Evil Eye Prayer"	27
Childhood	30
Be Grateful You Are Not the Gatekeepers	69
Remember Who You Are and Why You're Here	75
"Karma Said"	85
You Were God's Choice	92
You Were the Gift	95
"The Nature of Deception"	104
You Cannot Run from Karma	109
So, I Do Believe in Miracles	123
The Watchman Never Give Up: The Truth Is Always Revealed and Exposed	139

In *Ripley's Believe It or Not*, the Truth Always Comes Out	149
The Watchmen	149
Criminal Law Condition of Terms	152
Let Your Light Shine to the Heavens, Universe, and Earth	154
Breaking Generational Curses	155
Healing Karma Across Lifetimes	155
Breaking Free from the Matrix	155
Connections versus Attachments	156
The History of Intellectual Property Theft	171
Let's Connect	**195**

Prologue

Many of us were destined to become spiritual leaders, spiritual teachers, and self-love coaches. In order to become an ascended master, you must know your soul's purpose is to help other souls evolve from darkness into the light.

A soul goes through many different tests, challenges, and cycles. When we go through life lessons, we learn from all types of people, places, and things. How you react is your Karma; how they react is theirs!

Prologue

Self-Love Journey

You learn from every cycle, situation, and season you have experienced on earth. When your soul ascends to an ascended master, you have mastered all emotional, physical, and spiritual challenges, which is not an easy task at all. In fact, you really have to mirror and reflect your dark shadow side. Many of us had to face really extreme dark cycles and traumatic experiences. We had no choice but to get up, show up, survive, and evolve. You are not a copycat; you are the original blueprint here to help humanity expand, transcend, and grow.

- The soul's purpose is to help others evolve, grow, transcend, and expand.
- Self-love and self-improvement

Melissa Foreman

Be the Change

When you're in your soul's purpose, you radiate a light and energy that attracts good or bad into your life. We all must learn from the toughest trials and tribulation and evolve. When you've gone through as many difficult situations as I have, you can speak in an authentic and genuine manner, and people trust you because they are going through similar trials.

Start to live every day as though it's your life, because we are never guaranteed another day. Be extremely grateful for the love of the most high God, universe, ancestors, spirit, and archangels to protect and guide you every day. Let your energy and light motivate and inspire others. And they will watch you to learn how to take steps to get to enlightenment.

Lead the way. God knows the trials and tribulation I had to face to get where I am today. I am a survivor, not a victim. I was given this position to lead others out, because there's no one else. I can tell you how to pick yourself back up. We are the key to healing ourselves through positivity, meditation, energy, love, joy, happiness, and light. Unless there was someone who had walked through the darkness, I had to defeat battles to get to the light.

No one can keep up with the same elevation. Tell yourself, "I love you. I love everything about you." The first step is gaining alignment in your life. It sounds easier said than done. This is one of the most difficult steps in the awakening process: to clear the mind of any thoughts, old patterns, habits, ingrained childhood wounding, life, funding, and survival triggers. You must cleanse these emotions out of your energy addictions, practice celibacy, eat healthy, and exercise. You must take care of your vessels and love yourself first. Get up and say, "I love you. I love everything about you." Look at yourself in the mirror and say this 10 times. Believe it with your soul. Our vessels were lent to us by God, and many of us abuse them with stress, eating poorly, and overall bad habits.

Come into power and be a blessing and role model to others. After the towers fall on your life, they're actually very cleansing, if you look at them. Towers exist when you ignore your intuition to change, improve, and get away from toxic people. Toxic behavior is toxic energy that brings you down. Towers exist to cleanse away the wrong path and the wrong direction. Every one of us goes through testing of the mind, body, and spirit via temptations, childhood wounding, traumas, and tribulations.

Energy is a binding force; protect it, and do not allow people in your energy that are not for your higher purpose or higher God. Release them out of your energy, or you'll attract them like magnets, either positive or negative. I know it's really hard sometimes because you really love people who are toxic, and you want to take care of everybody, but you have to take care and love yourself first before you can love anyone else. They drain your energy like energy vampires, and we have to cut the cords to any energy vampires that no longer serve a higher purpose. These people were sent to draw your energy to make you fail. Anyone who it makes you believe that you're not good enough is projecting their inner insecurities onto you. They feel like a failure due to addictions of drugs, sex, power, money, greed, temptations, and failure. That is a them problem, not a you problem. You cannot help everyone; you must first love yourself and focus on surrounding yourself with love, joy, happiness, peace, and protection at all times. It's okay to say no, especially when you know these individuals do not have or support your higher good. It's all energy exchange, so you will attract what you put out.

Energy is binding, so if you are not aware that being in someone's space with negative energy, you're carrying on their Karma and all the relationships and toxic behaviors they've endured over their lifetime. We are the gate keepers to our soul, so protect it at all times. This is your gateway to success to attract positive people and influences in your life and drop any negative behaviors and people, even if they are family or friends. Anyone who does not serve your higher good is considered an enemy, and if you're in a battle for your soul, why would you let the enemies in your house? Release the guilt of staying connected with toxic people. It opens a gateway every time you communicate.

When you know these are your enemies, that opens a portal, a gateway, and allows you to cut off that bad energy. You are not obligated to save them or redirect them. It's not about that. You must love yourself first and always think of yourself. I know this struggle seems difficult and self-centered, but if you don't take care of yourself, no one else will. No one else will care more than you care for your vessel, your soul, and your mind, body, and health. These same individuals will be in my life in the next year, three years, five years, 10 years. Let it go without guilt.

As a soul, we go through these challenges to evolve, learn, close toxic cycles and past lifetimes of Karmic debt, Karmic issues, and Karmic people. We do this by loving ourselves and transcending to the next best self. Pay attention to your intuition, your inner voice, and your inner thoughts to stay still. It's okay learn about yourself first. It's okay not to tell everyone your business; it isn't their business. They just want to know what you're doing to take it away, stop good things in your life, and take away your positive energy.

Energy vampires are real. You know this from when you feel exhausted after you're around them. Family friends, neighbors, coworkers: all of these people aren't for your higher good. You need time to heal from all your lifetime trials, tribulations, traumas, childhood, religious beliefs, society, dogma, false news, false politicians, governments, judicial systems, corruption, criminals, influences, drugs, exposures, kidnapping, premature son born 29 and a half weeks, deaf son, almost lost daughter during birth, multiple miscarriages , molestation, bullying, life-threatening injuries to husband after motorcycle accidents, loss of job, physical abuse, mental abuse, stalker with psychiatric illness, defamation, lies, harassment, abuse, harm, control, pain, sorrow, grief, need for power, status, greed, money beliefs, abandonment, loneliness, entire family conflict, mother marrying 10 times, family violence, family death due to cancer, grandmother death due to Covid, death, surviving a spouse death and attack on my family with a gun, guilt, having my children with an abusive, drug-addicted parent who mentally and physically abused us for years until he attacked our family, my children who stood up against their father to survive him, poverty, financial crisis left after death of a spouse, constant fear, lack of safety, can never trust anyone else but myself, physical trauma, jealousy, loss of freedom, loss of respect, loss of self, loss of love, loss of life, loss of strength, loss of foundation security, loss of hope, loss of faith, loss of youth, loss of abundance, loss of time and trauma of addictions, people who try to steal you.

The only real focus and power on this earth is from the most high God. Pray every day. Get on your knees and pray that you're grateful for another day. The Devil wants you to believe he is real, but who do you think he works for? God, the most high God. The Devil not real. He said to create illusions, and blockages get people off their path and journeys. Life controls you, but what did you participate in? That is an affirmation and is a good start. Look yourself in the mirror and say, "I love you. I believe in you and everything you are. I love you." Say it to people even though it's awkward. Hug them—hug therapy is a great therapy. It transfers love, light, and energy to another person's soul. Soul energies are really important. Tell people!

Transfer that positive energy to someone else by hugging them. Say, "I love you." The creator gave us our soul and heart to manifest anything. You must open your heart. Love forgives. Forgiveness is for you, not for the other person. How you react is your Karma; how they react is theirs. To manifest anything in your life, you must transfer energy and deposit it. Be an alchemist for your transcending energy. Everyone has his capability to do that. You have control of your vessel, your soul, your mind, and your heart.

Most of all, some of us have never been loved before. Really show you are healing by opening up all of your chakras. There are multiple chakras on your body. This allows you to manifest energy into your vessel ,your soul, your mind, and your body. You are the gateway captain of your soul. Love yourself first, forgive others and yourself, and pray to get out of the darkness every day. You get up show up every day, brush your hair, brush your teeth, be grateful for the broth you have in your body, thank the people that are your true soul, try let go of toxicity, and forgive yourself for the past—the past life, Karma, addictions, bad life choices, and wrong journeys.

Forgive yourself, and forgive them; that's the hardest thing, to forgive them and let go and without guilt, remorse, or grief. To let go, your soul must transcend, and it does that through the heart. The heart is your most important organ in your body. Love your heart yourself, as it controls everything around you and attracts positive and negative energy. Open your heart. I have lived in the shadow of darkness and wanted to give up praying to God every day, but I was not really realizing that I am protected. I am safe, and I was allowed to experience life lessons, but it's us who have to either learn from these lessons and cycles and move on, or repeat them over and over and over.

In this lifetime, I chose to just move forward and help others do the same. Since I was five, I've had these abilities to see things with clarity and know things before they actually happened. I was 345 and not understanding my abilities. I was given dreams to learn. I did not have a mentor myself at all in this lifetime to learn about these gifts. I remember when the movie *The Sixth Sense* came out, and I was recalling that, wow, there's other people like me. It made sense to me, like I could see things or people or dreams and it was not my mind playing tricks.

I knew things when I was a young girl, and what happened to me tested me because I was given these gifts of clarity, healing, and knowing my purpose here. I am God-built and a warrior for Him of truth, and I have the ability to alchemize using my energy to manifest anything in my life. Wrongdoings and injustices are exposed to me. That is a part of a contract that I have with the divine, to help others transcend, learn to heal, direct humanity from all the dogma, matrix ideas, and beliefs, and expose corruption and wrongdoings. I am a truth fighter for this world, and no one knows who to follow or how to lead us out of the chaos of generational curses and wars.

I was given the gifts of clarity, healing, light, love, joy, and happiness, but also the gifts to use my energy to detect and fuel other people's energy, good or bad. There's a certain vibration with every human being. If you're at a high vibration, you are not tempted by anything negative, like addictions of alcohol, drugs, sex, and greed. That's not the right way, to manifest those things in your life; you must first start with healing yourself, your soul, your mind, and your body to attract and manifest everything you desire.

Your life starts with you; it's within you. It's not because of anyone else. You are the captain of your vessel. You are the navigator of your vessel. You are the gate keeper of your heart, mind, body, and soul. No one else can do these things for you. Once you release that understanding, you can start. None of these things can manipulate you except yourself. It's all about you, and when you forgive, move on, and heal yourself, you will realize that God made you go through every single thing. Every one of you has gone through it, so I can share my experiences of how I overcame disparity, death, sickness, and illness in my friends, family, and enemies because of my spiritual gifts.

That is my purpose here: to share my life with you and teach you how to manifest out of the darkness so you can receive the gifts and rewards that you were meant to have on this earth, in this realm. I have gone through every single horrible event in my life. Many of you know about this, and I will discuss them in these following pages so you understand that I speak from experience. Knowledge, understanding, and heartfelt healing messages will manifest your dreams. Even in the times of darkness, don't give up ever. Think of it as a matrix. This is not reality; it's an illusion, and we are tested with temptations, challenges, trials, and tribulations along the journey. There are evil people put on the paths to deter you from your Karmic journey.

Step One

You used to love yourself and say, "I forgive you. You are not awoken, you did not know. If you do not show them forgiveness, none will be shown to you."

A manifestation journal is important as you go through the awakening and transcending of your soul. Get a journal and write down all of your thoughts and ideas, good or bad, and surround yourself with positive energy and manifestations. Every day, meditate. Meditate. Meditate. It is really hard in the very first training of your mind not to have any thoughts, no thoughts at all. Start with five minutes. It gets easier. Your thoughts manifest into reality, good or bad. It's a magnet. What you say, think, and do is energy, or an energy exchange, so you have to learn to control yourself. Get out your thoughts and ideas first. Ask for protection.

I am grateful as above, so below. I ask for healing of my heart. I ask for deliverance from whatever is blocking or hindering my success to what God has planned for me. In the name of the most high God spirit, God universe, and ancestors, every person I release and ask for deliverance. I release the Devil and demons and ask God, the anointed Holy Spirit in the name of the most high God spirit, God universe, they must return to sender, return to owner, let it backfire into their life, their home, their reality. I return anything that was stolen from me. I break the contract of trauma, tribulation, trials, childhood bonding, addictions, physical abuse, psychological abuse, mental abuse, spiritual abuse, molestation, marriages that are toxic, relationships that are toxic, friends, family, and neighbors, people that are toxic and jealous. Let it return to sender, let it return those contracts.

I command in the name of God to go back to the sender. We break it now; I command what has been given by God to be loose to be released and returned to me 10 times more than what I lost. In the name of God, I thank you for releasing whatever entangled my finances. We break the power of the evil ones off from my life off of my finances, we cut the energy vampire courts, we cut them, we break the power of the evil one off of my life in God's name. Let the glory and the spirit of God, the universe, and my ancestors touch my finances and my life in the name of Jesus., along with any adversity that gave the evil one's legal ground to negate what was rightfully mine.

In the name of God, we break the power, we break the courts, we cut down anyone that is evil in my life, we cut the courts. God, teach me how to prosper. Show me, teach me how to believe in miracles and have faith. Today is my last day in poverty. We take authority of the brethren, we decree the release of financial bonding and the release of any witchcraft. We decree the release of financial bandages, the release of all witchcraft, juju, voodoo, heck does curses, black magic Saturday, then goma Obeah, every form of witchcraft 010 agua, every four we break it, and we returned to sender, in the name of God, the spirit, the universe, and our ancestors. I take authority over my finances, and I break the evil power over my family, life, and finances, of darkness that has blocked my finances, my extreme lock abundances, extreme wealth, prosperity, generational wealth, limitlessness, a bun, gifts from universe, and the Merritt goddess ancestors that visited me. I take authority of any witchcraft that has been blocking my finances. I take authority of any spirit of the devouring that has been destroying my luck and my money. My limitless abundance is limitless, finances limitless, resources limitless, wealth, we destroy any witchcraft, any money-altering spirit, Texas curses of my life, my family's life. We break any agreement, a party, with my enemy, the Antidikos.

Daily Prayers of Protection

"Archangel Michael," I ask you to protect me, my home, my finances, my family, my vehicles, and my opportunities with your powerful shield. Surround us with your purple light, which allows only pure love to penetrate. Please stay with me day and night and keep me and my loved ones safe. Love you—as above, so below.

There are over 16 archangels: Michael, Rafael, Gabriel, Uriel, Soryal, Raquel, Remeao, Metatron, Camille, Hania, Casio, that kill joe feel Sandahl, Raziel, and Bezaleel. We are born with soul guides, spirit, ancestors, guides to protect us on our journey and path, and of course, the most high God.

Step two: start walking, exercising, taking care of your vessel, eating healthy, meditating, and praying every day. Start paying attention in your journal to science and synchronicities numbers and symbols. When you start elevating to a higher level, that type of communication comes in frequently in your dreams and in your mind on a daily basis. That means you're on the right path, you're happy and vibrating high, and these communications are coming in to help you and guide you. Pay attention. Use your manifestation journal to research signs and synchronicities.

Let's just be honest: these enemies do exist and are put on your path to test you tempt you. These trials and tribulations are led by people who are at a very low vibration, which means they are there to attack you, break you down, demolish you, and destroy you, so when you pray, pray for yourself and your family to be protected. Father God, I pray that these lost souls that have attacked me and my family will find the light of Jesus, in the mighty name of the Lord God.

Jesus Christ, I was just trying to blow up all walls of protection around any of those witches and witches' covens, colton's warlocks, withers magicians, Karmics, spirituals, haters, false prophets, devils, demons, cults, satanists, and narcissists, and break and destroy the power of the curses in hexes and black magic, voodoo, juju graveyard, santería, and gomaa, witch caster, vexes, spells, charms, fetishes, voodoo dolls, psychic prayer, psychic thoughts on witchcraft, rituals, cords, magic, candles, sorcery, all mind control, jinxes, potions, in devil's den demonics. Return to sender all the bewitchment, death spells, destruction, spouse chaos, paul's, ask isabel, sickness, spell, painesville torments valve, psychic power, warfare, prayer chains, and everything else that was sent my way. My life and my family members, my possessions, money, wealth, opportunities, let it backfire, let it return to sender, let it return to the owner. Amen. I break those rituals, I break those isolation, spells, sorrow, grief. I don't care what type of religious background you are, demons, devils, witches, warlocks, magicians, practitioners, and toxic energies.

Father God, in the Lord Jesus Christ's name, please send your warrior angels to surround me and protect us, surround me with your radiant light, Lord, and cleanse me from spiritual impurities, show me from harm, remove any curses that may have been cast and release me from their grip. Let your love, light, and grace feel every corner of my being, banishing all darkness and fear. I declare my faith in you, God, as my ultimate protector and savior. Strengthen my spirit and guide me on the path of righteousness. Grant me the wisdom to discern the forces of darkness and the strength to resist influence.

These demonic spirits are real and will attack you. If you were at a low vibration or energy exchange, remember that when you're on a higher vibration, you will never be subject to these types of entities, like demons, devils, witches, witches' covens, Illuminatis, secret societies, and false religious leaders. Raise your vibration and return to sender every day, morning and night.

"Evil Eye Prayer"

I called back my power. I called back my energy. I sever all ties to toxic energy, people that no longer serve my purpose, and God made it so those who bring ill intent never affect me. Any evil eye turns blind at the sight of me. Make it be returned. Reflective times three, no ill will against me shall prosper. I am protected and loved by the forces that be, as I will, so mote it be. Protection prayers are a daily part of my life.

Every night, I say the Lord's prayer: our Father, who art in heaven, hallowed be thy name, thy kingdom come thy will be done on earth as it is in heaven, give us his daily bread, and forgive those who trespass, and those who trespass against us. Please deliver us from any evil, as above, so below. Amen.

Now I lay me down to sleep, and if I die before I wake, I pray the Lord my soul to take.

Everything the enemy has stolen, God's going to restore: your peace, your sleep, your joy, your health, your family, your finances, Amen. As above, so below.

Behold, I give unto your power to try to pond snakes, serpents, and scorpions, and over all the power of the enemy, and nothing shall by any means hurt you. I am strong. I am strong. I am strong by the Lord. I praise you. You are holy, you are holy, you are holy. I am in need of your supernatural powers. Once again, I know that no darkness can withstand the power of your light, and no harm can befall me under your shelter of your love. I ask you to break and dispel any effects of witchcraft that have been cast upon me and against me and my family. I remove all the negative influences and the power they may have had over my life, in the name of Jesus Christ, and through the intercross of Archangel Michael. I call upon the divine protection, Father God in the name of Jesus Christ. Please send your angels to surround us and protect us.

Close the window, close the gate, close the door, never open it again, seal it tight, protect me and myself. I am strong and healed. I am strong and healed. I am strong and healed. Close the astral travel gate, close the door to the dream state astral projection. It ends today.

When you see signs in synchronicities of symbols, numbers, and patterns, pay attention to your angels and guides speaking to you, warning you. Pay attention. This is your compass to know the red flags along the path.

11:11: This number is an angel number symbol symbolizing new beginnings. When seen, it could mean that new opportunities are waiting for your right around the corner .

12:12: This number is an angel number. Angel number 1212 guides you to believe in prosperity and contentment. Joy is around the corner. This is a great positive sign that you're about to receive it.

Energy is the key to prosperity, abundance, love, light, and everything positive in your life

Remember, not everyone will heal in this lifetime, because some of us will not love to capacity or have the capacity to heal. Too much has happened on this journey and this path, too much is Karma dead, and there is no possibility of transformation. You cannot lighten or lesson Karma if you try, so then you take on that Karmic debt, which burdens you if you chose not to heal. You cannot blame it on Karma; it was you your choices you made, and you cannot play the victim. If you are on a high frequency, don't get too close, because you're going to be drowned in the waves. Everything is recorded in Akashic records by Archangel Metatron. Nothing is messed in this lifetime; everything is recorded from the moment you enter this world's matrix until your demise. Judgment is performed at spiritual court, and our hearts are measured. Did you fulfill the contracts assigned to you? All evidence is brought, and all lies deception, defamation, universal spiritual judicial logic broken, are brought to court. Did you fulfill then you get to go to the kingdom?

If not, then judgment is made. Do you have Karmic debt which will be paid out in future lives? It's not guaranteed to pay that Karmic debt. Sometimes if you are evil towards anyone here on this round, you're not given another opportunity, and your jail/prison time is permanent purgatory. There is no way to cheat your way into heaven; either do the work or be judged at the end of your life. It's your choice. You had time on this journey to ascend your soul, to evolve to your higher purpose. In a lifetime, it goes by in Karmic cycles of seven years. You were weighed and measured and either have a Karmic debt, or you prosper and broke generational curses or your lineage. Do not try to save someone from their own Karma. Otherwise, you will carry their burdens. Not everyone is granted spiritual protection and gifts.

How did you help humanity? My purpose is to heal others, and now I am a master 33 top-tier energy healer and spiritual teaching warrior of truth and corruption.

Every person and relationship up to this point was teaching us a lesson. What the lesson is is where you have to do your homework. Did you really learn it? We are tested during this entire lifetime to make sure we have surpassed God's gaze, which is reflected in your heart at the end of this journey. Don't let outside influences affect your mood. You are here to help humanity, evolve, and transform and transcend proof. Good people do exist without hidden agendas. Be consistent. The fakes will always come to light. Just give it time. You are the original blueprint, not a copycat. The awakened is the most powerful energy to mirror for the lost souls. It is the level of clarity you bring to their life. You inspire others to reach their highest potential and also have the ability to hold space for the dark shadows.

So you can understand me, my life has been a *Dateline* movie since I could even remember being conscious and aware at two years old of my environment. I am going to tell you in detail my story, my life's trials, tribulations, and despair. It is not the bed of roses in the Cinderella story everyone thinks I lived.

Childhood

When I was two years old, I remember getting hit on the forehead with an abrupt blow that knocked me over in my highchair because I didn't want to eat brussels sprouts. I immediately started having seizures and other childhood calamities, like strep throat. I was allergic to antibiotics and had kidney infections, urinary tract infections, fevers, chills, and high fevers. By the time I was five, I was in the hospital with dialysis. I thought I knew that there were dark dreams I was having, and I can recall things from my past and ask my angels for help, guidance, and protection.

My mother had married 10 times, so we were frequently moving homes. We moved at least five times in my kindergarten year and twice yearly after that. Every family member used drugs and physically hit and beat us. I also saw my mother go through that abuse. She smoked, and at the ages of 3–10 years old, I was left alone every day and was a victim of molestation by my grandfather, uncles, and friends, who were alcoholic. To soothe myself, I rocked myself in my bed and cried often. Even then, isolation for me was comfortable and felt normal. It was better than the chaos that surround me every day of my life. There was never a point at which I did not live in survival mode or the emergency lane. I always had to protect myself and my family from pedophiles, abusers, and addiction, and I had to run for my life.

I never felt comfortable in a safe home or environment my entire life. I remember at a young age predicting things and telling my friends and family, who thought I was crazy. Then, the dream would come true. I felt my angels all the time. The energy of the angels was with me. I never felt darkness or lost my way, because I was an observer of life. I was watching it happen around me and to me, but not owning it that is a choice. You are not a product of your environment. Everyone has a choice, and no matter how bad it is, you have the choice to make a different alternative decision. It's easy to blame others who treated you badly in life, but you have to take accountability for why the lesson was there for you. If you did not learn it, and you had to remain in that cycle.

I always felt like it was a curse. This was not my family. This was not me. This was not my life. Car accidents, multiple bouts of pneumonia and Covid, surgeries to remove a cysts, miscarriage, living my entire life in violence and in the emergency lane, survival mode, car accidents, death threats, running for my life from my husband with a gun who tried to kill my entire family. I only survived because we had to fight. We had no choice but to survive that attack. We had to fight. Warriors never give up, even against drug-addicted people, jealousy, envy, narcissists, broken hearts, bullying, harassment, isolation, grief, sorrow, betrayal, thieves, depression, and stress. I thought to pull myself up, and I survived. My angels, who are the reason I was saved from every single situation, especially when my husband tried to kill me, protected me and my children from harm. You have choices: either give up, or stand up and be a warrior.

You set the trends, and they follow them. You can rewrite history, your history, your story. If they try to copy you, that means you're doing something right. We are the pioneers, the initiators and leaders. You can be a sheep, or you can take the world by the horns and be a fierce leader. You are the game changer. You never will have somebody give you handouts. The crown is permanent; you're a boss. There is nothing wrong with knowing your self-worth and experiencing self-love. Be confident. No one can be you better than you.

Energy is my first language. I understand it more than i do my own words. Energy has the power to change everything in your life and attract positive and negative energy into your life. Spirit, God, the universe, and angels and ancestors have protected me so I could feel God's mission. Since I was a child living through horrific circumstances, violence, physical abuse, mental abuse, and sexual abuse, I never ever lost my belief in God. I never gave up, even though it made me mad, upset, and angry at times. Why me? What did I do to deserve this type of life? I often was just a lone and isolated, abandoned by friends and family. Downloads and dreams started coming when I was a child, and they really helped me to understand that there was something coming, something else. It gave me hope.

Every person in my life but God has disappointed me with viciousness, lies, stealing, cheating, rumors, slander, bullying, harassment, defamation of character, hostility towards me and my family, and gossip. These were people who hurt and abused, me coworkers who destroyed my life out of envy and jealousy of my spiritual life and God's gifts. Not one person could I trust in this lifetime. My point is this: you can never give up. Find the light in every day so you can get up and show up. Every family member I ever trust end up betraying me, abandoning me, and leaving me behind. I lived my entire life in the emergency survival lane, fighting everyone's belief system and religious system, standing up for my rights, letting go of the darkness, breaking the chains and chords on my life for my freedom, and cherishing every single day. People who made up lies will be exposed when the truth is revealed.

You have to learn to love yourself love authentically first; you can't wait on anyone else or a knight in shining armor to come rescue you. I was so used to the disappointment in everyone that I could read their energy when they were being deceitful to me. Every day I woke up, and I had to look for something light, fun, joyful, happy, and humorous to entertain myself and love myself, because no one else cared about me or if I survived. It was up to me to survive and fight. Because I was physically hurt and mentally abused my entire life, I had to self-sooth and heal myself.

That is how I knew I was a healer, because I could heal my suffering. I could heal my walls and kill the pain that was trying to kill me, poisoning me with broken hearts, pain, sickness, diseases, mental illnesses, broken dreams, depression, broken bones, three miscarriages to delivery of children in the second trimester, placenta previa in my firstborn child who was 10 1/2 weeks premature in the hospital for three months. He was born 3 lbs, 2 oz, and I had to go to the hospital every single day and feed my own child for survival. My daughter was born not breathing, and they had to almost break her shoulder to get her out. My youngest son was born deaf. We had learned he was deaf when he was 16 months old, and I had to put him on a bus in a car seat to go to school for the deaf to help him learn to sign. All the wounds were deep, the bleeding, pneumonia, thyroid condition, losing my hair to stress, breast cyst, ovarian cyst, Covid, hives, allergic reaction, antibiotics, anti-lactic shock, strep throat, infections, kidney infections, husband after he tried to kill me with a gun, husband's a motorcycle injury that caused him severe damage and pain due to head injuries. Fractures, mental illness, not having a financial plan or backup, almost bankrupting me and my family, a hostile workplace environment due to jealous people during a time in which I really needed someone in my life to deliver me from the darkness, accidents, job loss, job change, college, grief, drugs and alcohol, addiction of everyone in my family, abandonment, physical, beating, sexual molestation by my grandfather and other close family members, rape, never feeling safe, homelessness, living in a car, betrayals, cheating, lies, violence, hunger, poverty, stressors, verbal abuse, almost drowning, temptations, and a DNA test proving a family scandal that my grandfather is not my real grandpa.

Your entire belief system is turned upside down, and you don't know who you are or believe where you are. This is from hostility, the loss of people I truly loved, the constant disappointments, obstacles blockages, hurdles, feeling of drowning, and the mountains I had to climb being a woman in a leadership position. These heavy burdens and trials all were meant to trigger me. People only viewed me on the outside and would judge me, but they didn't know all of the true shit show I endured my entire life since I was been born and that was bestowed upon me. I never gave up. Who is ever going to come and rescue me but God, my angels, spirit, and universe. It was not an option to give up. I am a warrior, a truth fighter, and a right fighter for injustices. I have never thought of ending my life. I never thought of giving up, stopping, or allowing the enemy to win. It was up to me to find the light and healing, and I learned the art and victory of truly loving myself first. The truth is always revealed; they are no match for you. You need to learn to authentically love yourself, respect yourself and honor yourself. So, I support the team that proves you are not a product of your environment. You have choices. Sometimes life stings, but trust in the spirit that there is a plan. I know you're helping others heal.

Every secret is eventually exposed. Nothing is ever had, and the truth always comes out. Surrender to complete healing, a partnership that leads to marriage, and a windfall of abundance that leads us toward your life's purpose. The biggest betrayal in love leads you to your biggest blessings.

Don't ever let anyone else tell you your gift is evil. Definition and prophecy exist ;deal with it. They demonize your spirituality and gifts because these things are powerful, and they don't want you using them to help heal others. Nobody can see you for the table God set for you. You are an incredible woman; don't ever doubt yourself. I had to become a fearless leader, and this is the energy I needed for my success. Remember that when you have the opportunity to help someone, do it, because that's the universe telling you or answering someone else's prayer through you. I know I have had guardian angels with me my entire life. People have always just tried to block me, and I've had to tear down the doors.

Hidden agendas were revealed where people misused their control and power. A company involved in money laundering, a case from the past, was deliberately sabotaged to discredit any of my work. In a future case that involves me, they were soliciting others to sabotage me on my path. They were angry their dealings and wrongdoings were getting exposed. These are liars who have no integrity and believe they are an elite group of wealthy people, but the reality is, they're just criminals with gay-for-pay platforms, judges who own judicial systems, prostitution, drug addictions, alcohol, sexual addictions, and gambling. These high-line criminals are involved in money, group sex, cult sacrifices and rituals, Illuminati, laundering, theft, identity theft, OnlyFans websites, the dark web, swingers, sex parties with underage children, pedophiles, witches, warlocks, coven cults who pay for and use magicians, and accountants who perform spiritual warfare. They are dove devils in demon satanist narcissists who live in this lifestyle of corruption and break and destroy all the powers by doing curses in hexes and black magic, voodoo, juju graveyard, santería, goma, witch casters, vexes, spells, charms, fetishes, psychics, prayers. All witchcraft, rituals, cord magic, candle magic, sorcery, magic ball mind control, jinxes potions, contaminated food and drinks, are demonic. Return all to sender, by which means death spells, destruction, spells, chaos, spells, accidents spell, sickness, pain, torment, love, spells, sex spells, physical power, physical warfare, per change, and everything else, all to control and hide this secret society, Illuminati, and false religion. Religious followers pray in church on their knees and go home and use magic, black magic, voodoo, and any type of magic by practitioners who are paid to take out people, steal their money, get them under illusions and spell work, and take what they want from them.

These people attacked me at work, called my employer, blocked my work opportunity, slandered me and my family, wished death, chaos, harm, car accidents, lack of money and finances, broke my ribs, made me fall, and wished sickness death on me and my family. For eight years, I was subject to a tyrant and his group of toxic friends and family. He knew I knew his truth, and his family and friends told him, and that is why he attached to me; because he owed me money. He didn't have a relationship with me for two and a half years, but he ended up being paid to gaslight me for two and a half years by the Illuminati's secret society. Then, he ghosted me completely and never spoke to me again. He was hiding his drug addiction and sexual addictions. He was married to a witch in the witches' coven, and he was bisexual and had a relationship with the man the entire time.

God sent me and to try to help this person, awaken his soul, to get him on the path. We talked about it frequently, but it really was just a set up. He acted as though he was my friend and betrayed me. He acted like he was in love with me and betrayed me with a friend at work, friends I grew up with, coworkers, and family. He slept with them because he did not want to commit, which is actually a blessing in disguise. I pray, and I'm grateful every single day that I listen to God's guidance. Every single day I was protected by my angels from the tyrant Devil because he knew honestly that I had these gifts, and I would expose them all publicly and shame them with the truth.

He called my previous employer and blocked over 4000 applications and 400 job opportunities. He called an employer and told them that I was psychiatric and was worried about me working with patients, so i was let go from that position. He and his group of haters constantly stalked me. I made several employer complaints and contacted attorneys for online stocking, slander, defamation, and bullying an entire company along with me. He ruined my 29-year career to cause me pain, to cause me grief and stress. Isolation was their idea to cause depression. I experienced anxiety and loneliness because I refused to go back to this person. After learning all of these dirty things these people were involved in—I was not involved in threesomes or group sex parties, travel agencies, prostitution, and this culture of non-stop partying—I was told I was too boring for this person because I was not about living in the OnlyFans pages, hedonism, drugs, couple swapping, same-sex encounters, oral cult things, rituals, and sacrifices. He slept with people I worked with and convinced them that I was against filing a lawsuit. There were video recordings, texts, emails, and letters regarding the harassment I received by this group of haters driven by this person. This person was purposely trying to ruin my life because I believed in God. He is my boss, not the devils, not the demons, not the Karmics. I belong to God; He is my boss. I report to Him.

My entire family was attacked, and I had to learn how to protect my family and myself using God's prayers to fight back and return to sender any of the chances, spells, the enchantments, the witchcraft, cutting cords, everything by the wicked ones. I had to return to the sender every single day for eight years. I was attacked in every satanic town. I had to return every narcissist that I came across. In the mighty name of God and Jesus, I had to return it back any sort of deas or satanic thought? I return it back to them. I had to return it back in the name of Jesus. It will backfire on your head, every wicked thought will backfire on your head, anything, let it backfire on your head in the mighty name of Jesus. If you sent any wickedness towards me, or my family, my business, to end my life or my children's lives, let it backfire on you. Let you stumble, let you fall, let you die. Everyone seeking after my life, let them all stumble. Anyone wishing I die or end my life, you will die. It had to be returned to sender.

I was attacked every single night for eight years by these wicked people. They tried to block my luck and my gifts from the spirit, God ancestors, anything that was spiritually in alignment for me to receive my prosperity, abundance, and luck. They blocked me, and I had to return it and let it backfire on them. If they prayed for me to die, they had to die. Let them seek after my life or fall, and let them all fall. Anyone that sought to end my life, in the mighty name of Jesus, we cut the cord to the energy vampires. The witch is using enchantments against me, so I command your spouse to work against you now. Amen. To witches using spells and charms, we cut the cords; we cut the cords to the energy vampires and enchantments against me. I can bend your spouse to work and kiss you now.

For any satanic spells or demonic spells that you were sending against me which cross paths, I command those spirits to return back and attack you in the mighty name of Jesus. I command those supposed to work against you, every enchantment fighting me or my family, let it backfire on you. Return to sender. I command it. Every wicked witch, send her spouse to me and my family. I command it all, all the spells in your sentence to work against you, return to sender. I command it works against you now, the wicked witch is falling and dying pursuing me wherever I go. Die in the mighty name of Jesus, wicked witches who pursue me everywhere. i go for him die if you sent work to work business, a business family to family, narcissist, narcissist, texas taxes In the name of Jesus, amen.

I pour back my energy, and I poison the thieves, and I allow the most high God to take control. You are not ordained, wicked witch, so you need a trap for me; let it trap you and destroy you and your household, and you die. Any wicked witch setting a trap for me let it trap you and destroy you and your household and die. In the mighty name of Jesus, any traps sent for me, my work, my family, my money, business life, every cent, any trap you thought you set for me will trap you and your household, and you are returned to sender in the mighty name of Jesus. I pull back my energy, and I poison the thieves, and I allow the most high God to take control. A man, a wicked witch is fighting my family ancestors. God is tracking them; now, be set in forever confusion, and be returned to you and your family.

Anyone doing wickedness towards me, let it return to you in the mighty name of Jesus. I return it back to you, back to the owner. Any disappointments, spirit, I return to sender; any sheen, I return to sender. I shall overcome dark forces in my life. I shall overcome any dark forces in my life. As the lord lives, I live, and I take authority in the mighty name of God, most high God, spirit, universe, ancestors.

I take authority over my finances. I break the power over my family and my life. I break any darkness that has blocked my finances, extreme luck, extreme wealth, prosperity, abundance, inheritance, legacy, generational wealth, and gifts from the universe. Spirit and ancestors, I take authority of any witchcraft that has been blocking me in my finances and my family I take authority of any spirit of the devouring that has been destroying me. We destroy any witchcraft and money-altering curses on my life and my family's lives. We break the agreement of poverty with my enemy because my adversity gives him the legal grounds to take what is rightfully mine.

In the name of God, we break the power of the energy vampire. We cut those cords in the evil ones, anyone not serving our higher purpose or good. We cut the chords forever. God, teach me how to prosper. Show me, teach me how to give. I believe in miracles, and I have faith. Today is my last day in poverty. We take authority of the accuser of the brethren, and we decree they release any witchcraft. We decree the release of financial bandages, the release of all witchcraft, voodoo, voodoo dolls, hexes, curses, black magic, graveyard magic, obeah, and every form of witchcraft. We cut those cords of the energy vampires. We cut it now, we break it from anyone who is no longer serving our good and our purpose.

I command what has been given by God to be loose, to be released and return to me 10 times more than I lost. In the name of God, I thank you for releasing whatever entangled my finances. We break the power of the evil over my life and my finances. We cut those cords. We cut them to the energy vampires and anyone no longer serving our higher purpose and good. I'll pull back my energy and poison the thieves, and I will allow the most high God to take control. Break the power of the evil one off of my life in God's name. Let the glory of the spirit, God, universe, and sister charge my finances and my life, in the name of Jesus, amen.

We close the window, close the gate, and close the door, never to open it again to anyone from the past. We protect ourselves and seal it tight. No one can enter. I am strong and healed. I am strong and healed. I am strong and healed. Close the ice or travel gate, close the door to my dream state. You are not allowed in my energy. The enemy has stolen everything. God is going to restore your peace, your sleep, your joy, your health, your family, and your finances. Amen, as above, so below. I called back my power. I called back my energy and severed all ties to toxic energy. I made those who bring ill intent never affect me. Any evil eye turns blind at the sight of me. I am protected and loved by the forces that be, as I will, so mote it be.

Archangel Michael, I ask you to protect me, my home, my vehicle, my family, my finances, my legacy, my inheritance, and my abundance with your powerful shield. Surround us with your purple light, which allows only pure love to penetrate. Please stay with me day and night and keep me and my loved ones safe. Love you, as above, so below. Behold, I give unto your power to tread upon snakes, serpents, scorpions, devils, demons, witches, warlocks, and magicians. I give you power over the enemy, and nothing shall by any means hurt me, or my family. I am strong, I am strong, I am strong.

Father, Lord, I paid you. You are holy, you are holy, you are holy. I am in need of your supernatural powers. Once again, I know that no darkness can withstand the power of your light, and no harm can the follow me under the shelter of your love. I ask you to break the spells of witchcraft that have been cast against me or my family. I renounce any negative influence in the power it may have had over my life, in the name of Jesus Christ. Through the intercession of Archangel Michael, I call upon the divine protection, Father God, in my Lord Jesus Christ's name, please send your warrior angels to surround and protect us. Surround me with your radiant light, Lord, and cleanse me from spiritual impurities. Show me from harm. Remove any curses or spells that have been cast and release me from their crap. Let your love and grace feel every corner of my being, banishing all darkness in fear. I declare my faith in you, God, as my ultimate protector and savior. Strengthen my spirit and guide me on the path of righteousness. Grant me the wisdom to discern the forces of darkness and the strength to resist influence.

God laughs at the wicked ones living in disgrace and shame, for He knows their day is coming. Thank the most high God I chose the right team.

These same people planned and for your demise, and after all that betrayal, here you are. Energy can attack you when you're at low vibrational energy levels. To raise the level, love yourself. You are the mirror to your soul. You learned the lesson; forgive yourself and them and say, "I return to the owner, return to sender, and I call judgment on these people."

Protect your energy at all times. Crystals channel energy, which can make them an important part of your spiritual or healing practices. However, the stones can then hold onto that energy, which can impact how they work. Luckily, you can cleanse crystals with sage to help purge any remnants of that energy!

We are under spiritual attacks. Here are are some tools to help guide you.

1. Pray every day. These prayers are for protection

2. Place sea salt around the entire perimeter and your bed

3. Use tea leaves and crystal sets, including rose quartz, amethyst, citrine, black onyx, jade, tiger's eye, moonstone, and clear quartz. Use these crystals for a spirit-cleansing bath.

4. Clear your home, cars, and property lines. Light sage and blow it out, allowing the smoke to filter in the air. Do this day and night.

5. Light white candles and pray for protection from your most high God, universe, spirit, ancestors, and Archangel Michael. I am safe. I am protected. There is no black magic allowed on me or my family. You might not enter my dream state, astros travel, dream travel, and portal travel. You are not allowed. I pull back my energy, and I poison the thieves. You're not ordained, and I allow the most high God to take control.

6. Take a spiritual bath with sea salt, crystals, tea leaves, rose, chamomile, lavender, lemon, ginger, and herbs.

7. Listen to meditation daily. It helps relax your soul and heal your heart, mind, body and spirit.

8. Walk. Take daily walks outside in Mother Nature. Walk in the grass, sand, and dirt without any shoes on. Feel it through your feet. If you think about it, your feet have 100 different acupuncture points, so being barefoot outside in Mother Nature feeds your soul.

9. Practice yoga and stretching on a daily basis.

10. Be near water. The ocean, lakes, or pools are the best options to cleanse, restore, and rejuvenate. The ocean has natural saltwater; listen to the ions in the ocean. Put your feet in the sand and saltwater. While you bathe with saltwater, use crystals to help, cleanse, and balance

all of your chakras that are blocked. These blocked chakras are the cause of diseases, illnesses, sickness, and stress.

11. Go on nature walks.
12. Hug a tree.
13. Hug a person. Say, "I love you." Transfer your love and heart energy to others.
14. Eat a healthy, balanced diet. Drink daily water, as much water as you can to cleanse and purify.
15. Take daily doses of tumeric, magnesium, vitamin D, and green tea.
16. Practice self love. Once a month, treat yourself to massages, coffee, lashes, hair, nails, or whatever makes you feel beautiful. Do this for yourself before anyone else. Laugh often for a daily cleansing of your energy.

The journey is about learning to have a deep connection with your higher self and the most high God above anyone else. Cut away any other connection that does not serve your higher purpose. If a person betrays you, why are you ever going to go back to the abuse? Love yourself enough. Every single person in the Bible had to be in isolation to learn about themselves and learn who they were to God, the most high God. Every character in the Bible went through isolation to learn the lesson of self love and the connection with yourself. Love yourself more. You must protect your energy at all times; that means letting go of people who backstab you and lie to you. They do not have your best interest in mind, and they are jealous. Let them go.

People will try to re-enter your life like none of this shit happened, but it did. Do they feel like this happened so long ago that you're just going to forget about it? There will always be people who want to test you your temperature to see if you're really healed. It is crazy to think you would forget about what they did. A betrayal is a betrayal; you're not signing up for the arguments, wasted emotion, or energy. Just focus on your path, your mission your journey. You do not hold grudges anymore. It's the principle you're fighting for.

God says we must forgive the enemies, like Judas, because how you react is your Karma. It hurts to the core, but just believe in God and pray every single day that he will take away the pain. God does not put you through pain without a purpose. Most people who hurt you will never tell you the truth of how they betrayed you. They will take it to their grave, so don't ever expect an apology. It's not necessary for your self-healing, self-love journey. The same people will gaslight you and act like nothing's wrong, or they did nothing, or we're part of the treachery. There are Karmic records. You can't erase it ever. Everything we do on this earth is recorded, from the time we're born onward.

In order to attract your true divine counterpart, abundance, and gifts from universe, you must let go of the resentment. Release it, then forget it in order to get the rewards you deserve. Remember to protect your energy, so it's not necessary to have a discussion, get in their energy, or be near them to forgive. Cut the binding cords to the soul ties, or they will continue to pull on your energy. Just let it go. This will raise your frequency. Cut ties with everything in your path. It's not who you are today or the path for the future.

For me, it's the principle, the truth: they want you to forget, and they will take the trash to the graves. It could be a work situation, coworker, friend, family, or past soulmate that betrayed you and expected you to fight. In reflection, what you are really trying to fight for there is nothing; it was destroyed. Sign up for more drama, hate, lies, bullying, harassment, lack of accountability, defamation, threats on my life and my familly's lives, poverty, blocking of opportunities, stress, hostility, violence, gossip, and slander. There's nothing to go back to. Love yourself more. There was only 20 percent of your time that was not in frustration, hurt, and pain,.There was nothing but bad memories with this group and frenemies. Why would I ever sign up in my lifetime for suffering again with the same people?

I was fighting to stay in a low-vibration frequency after I thought so hard on the inner workings. The dark night of the soul forgiveness, and isolation is useful for learning about my self-love journey. No, I'm never going back. I release you, and I am unbothered. I respect people who tell the truth. Chose to love yourself first. Your self love is your superpower; it's your strength. To manifest anything in this lifetime, you must love yourself first. It's your superpower after you elevate yourself to a high-vibrating energy level.

Why would you allow anyone in your life who is not on your same level and sees things at a different light? Don't waste your energy. When you learn the art of detachment, letting go, moving on, stepping over, and learning the lesson, that's your superpower: to manifest anything in your life. Thank them for crossing your path and then letting you learn from them. I don't care if people have been in your life for years or a few months; use discernment and mindfulness. You do not need them in your energy. They are not willing to be completely honest with the part they played in the betrayal. I know everything before it manifests, so use discernment; if you're feeling sick, fearful, nervous, bitter, or frustrated, they are not for you. Let them go and do not let them pull on your emotions. Let them go.

Do not expect that things will be easy. If it's meant to be, it will be. Beware of the wolf in sheep's clothing. Use your intuition so that you're 10 steps ahead of everyone at all times. You see some of these people's Karma when you're at a higher vibration. When you needed them most, they abandoned you and stole money, time, and energy that you can never get back. It's their Karma to go through exactly what they put out in the universe. You don't get in the way of their Karma; it's their baggage, their burden to bear.

Remember, these are the same people who left you for dead on the road, killed you, refused to give help, caused pain and intentional hurt, attacked my family, made plans to kill me, ruined my career, and didn't care about me at all. You cannot take on their Karma in the next level of the journey with you. You take your seat and your love and compassion with you. Ask in your prayers for signs, synchronicity, guidance, help, and clarity in your dreams. There are consequences when divine law and universal law is broken; it can mot be undone. Your Karma is your judgement.

Continue to vibrate at a high level. Protect your energy, practice self love, pay attention to your intuition, and never let the past affect your life for future.

This chapter of my life is about knowing my worth, acting accordingly, and never settling for less. I know what I deserve.

Stop going back to where God has already healed you. When you realize God is never late, you wait differently.

I walk with truth, faith, integrity, and humanity. Many Christians say they are in faith, but they are actually counterfeits who masquerade as though they follow. They face you with either an authentic face or a counterfeit masquerading.

I have been baptized in nine different face of religion. I know the bible, every version, and I read it multiple times. I still light a candle in every church. I pray that people will find the light and joy and will love themselves most of all.

There is no one else but you on this self-love journey. No one else will love you more. You are your own superhero warrior. The Holy Spirit alerts me and sends me signs and synchronicities. I feel their energy; that's why I have to protect it at all times. There are evil practitioners out there, and I have a bomb spirit team. I come with a bomb-ass ancestors, universe, spirit, and angels team. I am being sent evil eyes, evil intentions and evil words. There's so many copycats out there trying to be me. Sometimes we go on these journeys because we signed a contract with God, and we either fulfill the contract and are rewarded, or we do not fill the contract.

I've always had these gifts and have been judged my entire life since I was a child, so I've been given guardian angels so that I can fulfill the contracts signed by me. I've always thought I was a right fighter for bullies who attacked me my entire life. You would think that they would grow up, but no, they still had a group of boys attacking me. When you go through trauma and painful experiences, it's hard not to lock it into your subconscious. You need to heal these feelings. Feel it, don't hide it. Talk about it, acknowledge, it release it. Most of the time, this is blocked in your breathing sacral chakra; release it, let it go. I struggle as many of us have.

Everyone can be in your lane, but not everyone can be in your energy or be your friend. When you elevate up so high, you're on a different frequency, and you can smell the BS from a mile away. They can't be in your lane when you're at a high level. They didn't make the cut. You know to take out the trash for yourself. Have an elevated energy, which means you're always protected. You can't just be friends with anyone. You can smell a snake a mile away, and your spirit guides will, too. They're already warning you to step away and go in another direction, because the universe and ancestors see them and the plots to harm you. Listen to your spirit team, God, angels, universe, and ancestors.

It's pointless, mindless conversation if they are not on your same level and elevation. People will try to befriend you only to use your energy, and they will try to sabotage your growth because of their jealousy, bitterness, ego, and rejection reresentment. Be mindful that people always make mistakes and create drama and chaos. Never underestimate me and try to use your low vibrational energy to ruin my life. When I am provoked, the warrior gene is let loose. Do not wake the sleeping giant; it is sleeping, not dead.

To find sweet, loving, gentle, calm peace, we have had to go through literal hell, the dark night of the soul, fear, breaking generational curses, fear of losing your life, no safety, constantly living in the emergency lane, being in survival mode, being triggered, and enduring the storm of whatever life threw at them, so the calmness is an earned victory and behavior. I call for judgment and allow the most high God to take control and to manifest divine wealth. We are the only healers of our stories, and we see it's reflection on our lives and the truth in lessons we learned.

Get to know yourself through self awareness. Avoid distractions, and remove the negativity. Lead by example through truth, intelligence, and integrity. You are the change. We are champions for ourselves through this self-love journey. Cast the net. Tell your story and your relatable experiences. My life has literally been a *Dateline* movie since I was born. I am a survivor, not a victim. I choose my path of joy, happiness, love, and peace. I refuse isolationism and sadness.

We are here for a human experience and to learn emotional intelligence. People try to use your energy, and you must be able to discern the difference. They will try to manipulate your power. Your soul will always try to change you, but the soul recognizes other soul tribesmen in a bigger group that helps others. The power is in how you heal. The mantra is, the more you have, the more power you have to control your life. The more you raise your vibration, the more you are aware of the dark shadows. Know what your triggers are not to avoid emotion, but to understand why they're there and move forward. It's not about racing forward to get through the emotional triggers. Know yourself. Love yourself. Be a confident social influencer. It matters if you stood up as a warrior for injustices, integrity, mercy, grace, forgiveness, compassion, humility, honesty, peace, and truth.

Karma is the justification that you reap what you sow, and everyone was tested. Be confident in your own self image and truly know your self worth. No, it's okay that you may not fit into a religious persona. You must be comfortable with what you do in your life and who you are. No one knows you like you know yourself, and they cannot judge your journey. Only the most high God can judge your journey at the end, and He knows your heart.

There are many reasons why Christians go to church. They go to pray to God, but do they really know God in their hearts? I can also recite several passages from the Bible and been baptized in nine different faiths. This does not get you any closer to God. He knows if you're authentic on your knees and praying to have a personal relationship with him. He knows the fakes, the false people, the false religious people; he knows you cannot fake the universe. You cannot fake the spirit and God. You cannot fake anyone; it's your job to use discernment, and when He rescues you from someone, never go back. You don't need to. You've already learned the journey or that part of the lesson, and it's time to move forward.

Elevate your self higher, to the highest level of energy, to attract and manifest. What you desire the most starts with your self love and the most high God's love, which is first seen through all the depression and the darkness, that sadness and grief and sorrow. You know there's always a rainbow at the end of the storm. Some storms are meant to destroy and clear a path so you can see clearly. If you're going to a tarot reader, sitting in church, praying, reading the Bible, and then going home to perform majic voodoo, then you're not of God. His gifts of light are given through Him, through his healers, and through love, light workers, spiritual gifts.

If you are using any of these methods, you are not of God. He who has not sin casts the first stone and is a hypocrite. Why are you copying others if you're in church, acting pius, and then going home, smoking and drinking? You're not living in the truth if you are go home, drinking and smoking ,and not living the truth. Find your own style in life; plagiarizing someone else's setup just to get views is not the way the world is meant to be. Be your own genuine self. You need to be your own authentic self, and you cannot ever be me because you can't compete where you don't compare. No one else is the boss of you except for God. No one else. It stops with Him. Your opinions do not matter, only your self love and your relationship with him. Doing this is actually Karmic behavior, not divine behavior.

That's the difference between doing things and love and light through God or faking it till you make it. We must balance practicality and spirituality. They will create the reality we're in. So, think about energy. The more you are around sadness, sorrow, and isolation, then you create that in your environment. Surround yourself with life and light. When you're around laughter, joy, and a fun atmosphere, that's what you manifest in your life. Your energy must be protected at all times. It drives who you are and what you can manifest within your own life.

Heal yourself first. If you love yourself, it is your shield, and it will backfire and return to sender. A Karmic is someone who refuses to learn the universal lesson. Everyone has a choice; you're not addictive, and if you choose not to learn the universal lessons, then you are Karmic, and you will never manifest anything divine in your life built on love, light, and God. You cannot fake being a Karmic with

God; he knows that the more you're taking the time, meditating, walking nature, feeling the grass, practicing yoga, eating well, and drinking water, dthe more balance you'll become. Be your own superhero. Walk in your own truth. Be your own movement.

It's extremely difficult not to blame others for external factors and problems they initiated. True leadership is rising above the negativity. It wasn't luck that got you this far! Consequences must be balanced, so before you react, think about every behaviorand decision you make or do not make. Actions taken have consequences. You can not save anyone from their mistakes and own actions.

Humanity is tested every day. We must find our purpose and live it every day with passion. It's how you react that's your Karma. Through life lessons, we learn from our mistakes and motivate ourselves to become better people. An inspirational leader inspires teams to achieve great things.

The most difficult moments and life lessons shape who you are today. Lies, misinformation, false accusations, bullying, defamation of character, hatred, slander, and harassment define your character. How you treat others is always exposed through Karma. As leader, did you participate with integrity and honesty or act out based on deceit? Everything is always a choice.

Be a leader that unites and inspires other people. Empower the people rather than just managing a team to achieving goals. You can front all you want, but the universe responds to the real you, not who you pretend to be. Your Karma is your justice. Do the right thing, even when no one watching.

I never forgot where I came from because these experiences shape who we are! True leadership is about empowering others to lead, not create outdated belief systems and followers. True leaders will teach you that the fire will burn you, and you learn from the mistakes.

The danger is following false narratives, organizations, and individuals who will not rescue you from the consequences and instead will push you into the fire. Beautiful things happen when you remove your self from negative things and people. You have to take accountability for your actions through Karma.

At some point, you knew it was wrong. A positive outcome equals positive change.

Navigate through these challenges and stay strong during these tough times. Just stay positive. Sometimes we must go through these storms in order to clear the path. Never, ever mistake kindness for weakness. Have the strength and emotional intelligence to overcome and cope.

Servant leadership style is an outdated concept and leadership style. You need to build performing teams, and the very first items on the list are setting a vision and building trust, depending on if you walk the walk and do what you say you're going to do!!!

It's hilarious when you conveniently forget the role you played and forget the consequences of your actions to hide behind secret societies, groups of haters, cultic belief of high morals, piety, principles, and those who wear masks of integrity and innocent victims.

Did you forget the truth about the betrayals, deceit, destroying lies you told, hatred, guiding people down the wrong path, the obstacles and towers you orchestrated to gain power, status, and control, the promises you made for an illusion of high rank status or title, money, greed of materialistic things, bribes, and hedonism you used to manipulate and steal innovation and opportunities?

When God has his hands on you, he will handle the people who put their mouth on you. Karma must be balanced. As a leader, strive to be the author and innovator of your own story—no one else's version of you matters. When you are not the innovator and originator of solutions and ideas, it's considered cheating and plagiarism. You will experience a series of unfortunate consequences for the defamation, bullying, slander, betrayal, ostracizing, lies, deception, injustice, deceit, stealing of some else's efforts, ideas, actions, self-mastery, discipline, and creation. It was to gain prestigious business interests, wealth, influence, contracts, and status for greed.

You cannot have rewards without efforts There are no shortcuts in life; you must do the work. It's like wanting the college degree without going to college, or it's like wanting the gold Olympic medal without doing absolutely anything for it.

In a world of corruption of a group for power, revenge, manipulation, lies, greed, status, bribes, and illusions of money, people wear a public mask to cover their wrongdoings. There is always proof and evidence. You cannot hide from judgement and Karma. Turn your pain into power. My tolerance has changed, and I am grateful for evolving. If you want to run with me, rise higher.

Don't let anyone devalue your self-worth. To inspire others, you truly have to heal yourself first. When you live authentically, you attract beautiful things, and when you vibrate higher, you attract what you want in life. Positive energy attracts positive energy, and negative energy attracts negative energy. It's like a ripple affect into the universe, and the scale of justice and Karma must be balanced. You will reap what you sow.

Beware of frenemies, a group of secret haters who would rather sink the entire ship, put rocks in a lifeboat, remove the paddles and life preserver, and do everything possible to cause the shipwreck, chart the ship off course to hide their participation in the plot of mutiny of deception, deceit, destruction, bullying, lies, purposely blocking opportunities, slander, defamation of character, harassment, out-of-control jealousy, envious behavior, a copycat-led hate group, and stealing proprietary information due to their own lack of innovation and authenticity. I am the unsinkable Molly Brown.

When you choose to forgive them, you take away their power. How you react is your Karma. The key elements to a community leader are always to tell the truth, practice honesty and integrity, act with justice, and respect accountability.

The truth always comes out. What corruption, criminal acts, and bribery did you participate in and accept? Hidden enemies are always exposed and must face the consequences. Karma and justice do not miss an address, country, city, or state. It never makes a mistake, and you can never hide from it.

As leaders, how can we justify intentional corruption, harassment, intimidation, coercion, causing harm towards anyone, any abuse, defamation, criminal negligence causing an injustice, allowing toxic behaviors, telling lies, ignoring and hiding evidence of wrongdoings, participating in blocking any advancement opportunities, participating in a public stoning while at their job, or participating in a conspiracy to throw rocks and hide their hands after they orchestrated the abusive practices?

If you participated in this type of toxic behavior, do you really think you should be rewarded? Universal justice and Karma must be balanced. Some Leaders are destined visionaries who help humanity transcend, grow, learn, evolve, inspire, empower, and motivate others. In time, the real will be separated from the fake. Stay consistent. You are proof that good people without hidden agendas do exist. I am not a copycat or someone you find twice. I am the original blueprint.

Some storms and towers come to clear the path for new beginnings. True leaders do not purposely put down obstacles, block occupation opportunities, create hurdles, create drama, or encourage immaturity, obsession, stalkers, sociopathic tendencies, malicious intent, hostility, toxicity, hatred, jealousy, viciousness, chaos, traps, confusion, ego, poor decisions, conflict, illusions, bullying, persecution, slander, theft, ruthlessness, discrimination, and defamation, guide people the wrong way, project failure, and cause war and fear. The laws of universe are spiritual and judicial, and God considers this behavior crimes of blasphemy, treason, judicial corruption, misconduct, criminal negligence, and violation of law. If the leaders choose not to transcend and awaken, then they will attract negative patterns in their lives with the same consequences.

Whoever participated and joined will receive the same judgment and Karma that they projected on others. You reap what you sow. Successful leaders transcend and heal humanity from darkness, suffering, and shadows by using light, love, peace, and joy and facilitate the success of others. They do not push them down, step on them, to get ahead. They build the foundation for the future.

Leaders know that universal law can never be broken, no matter what religions, cults, secret societies, organizations, judicial systems, political institutions, Illuminati come their way. These gruops believe they possess special enlightenment and knowledgeable wisdom. They believe they are an elite secret group of powerful people who can control and stop universal law before it occurs. Universal laws can never be changed.

This is absolutely true, especially when you're able to see with clarity who your enemies are and expose the community lies, payouts, bribes, spells, false and unfounded accusations in courtrooms, stolen documents from mail, stealing cell phones, cloning, creating illegal videos and surveillance, identity theft, and the corruption of government officials to hide criminal actions, false reports and claims for false cases, and judicial injustices by thieves for greed, status, money, and inheritance.

This corruption is to hide scale of greed, money, and status to control the wealth and power of an elite group of secret societies, corporations, cults, self-proclaimed religious leaders, brotherhoods, criminal organizations, covens, politicians, government officials, judicial authorities, law enforcement, and judges, who serve blackmail bribes and payouts to hide trafficking and corruption on the dark web.

True leaders do not purposely put up obstacles, block occupation opportunities, put up hurdles, create drama, immaturity, obsession, stalkers, sociopathic, malicious, hostility, hold toxicity, hatred, jealousy, vicious, create chaos, traps, confusion, bigoted, cause confusion, act with ego, poor decisions, conflict, illusions, bullying, persecution, purgery, slander, thief, ruthlessness, discrimination, defamation, guides people the wrongway, project failure, cause war and fear.

The laws of universe are spiritual and judicial, and God considers this behavior crimes of blasphemy, treason, judicial corruption, misconduct, criminal negligence, and violation of law. If the leaders choose not to transcend and awaken, then they will attract negative patterns in their lives with the same consequences.

Whoever participated and joined will receive the same judgment and Karma that they projected onto others, including chaos, death, depression, diseases, and illnesses. You reap what you sow. Successful leaders transcend and heal humanity from darkness, suffering, and shadows by using light, love, peace, and joy, and they facilitate the success of others and do not push them down or step on them to get ahead. They build the foundation for the future.

God knows that the trials and tribulations we go through make us who we are today. And when you're in your soul's purpose, you radiate light and energy, good or bad, into your life.

Live every day as though it's your last; we are never guaranteed another day. Be grateful. I chose to be a survivor, not a victim, and I was given this position to lead others out of the darkness because there is no one else to tell you how to get your stuff back up again.

True leaders walk in truth, integrity, humanity, and faith. During times of tribulation, are you a leader who walks in true faith, or a counterfeit who masquerades as a person of integrity who walks in authentic faith? Sometimes you just have to sit and think how blessed you are. Seriously! Self-love is a healing journey, and this chapter of my life is about knowing my worth, acting accordingly, and never settling for less, I know my worth.

The calmer you are, the clearer you think. Move with strategy, not with your emotions. Keep working on becoming the best version of you. Learning to love yourself is the secret to everything you desire.

Move away from opinion-based, unfounded, biased thinking, and always check your facts and sources. Never assume anything is true until you validate that the information is factual—always trust, but verify and ask for proof and evidence. Make sure the information and medical examination is accurate and performed by a professional in the field of study—not by a biased opinion, but based on facts. Expose the thieves who stole from you, false allegations, false accusations, fraudulent facts, bribery tactics with judiciary officials, and unlawful misconduct to win-false evidence claims. Take action.

Thank the universe, and do not worry about the opinions of others. Keep shining. Stay strong, kind blessed, grateful, and always authentic. Sometimes the best thing you can do is to not wonder and to practice in faith. Do not imagine, do not obsess; just breathe, and have faith that everything will work out. It's easy to judge. It's more difficult to understand, because understanding requires compassion, patience, and willingness to believe good hearts are misled and may choose deceitful people in their life.

You cannot hide from universal judgment. It is your Karma and must be balanced. Karma has no deadline .What you do and say will return to sender; it will backfire into you and your family. God will come through every time.

Time to unmask and expose the toxicity and corruption, bullying, intimidation, harm, hatred, conflict, cruelty, drama, suffering, discrimination from colleagues, frenemies, community leaders, judicial officials, and administrators who purposely creates a hostile workplace. The truth always wins. Karma is your judgment. Life is about how you treat others. Be humble and kind. If you're a little mysterious and weird, own it. There's no one like you. The right people like you for it.

As leaders, why don' we ask questions and think critically? Why do people fall for false leaders, gurus, religions, and cults? It's because the true teachings ask for them to look inside and face all aspects of their shadow side. They want you to believe there's a faster way of digging inside themselves instead of accepting what the universe is presenting to them. They want to bend the rules. False leaders tell them they can; however, a true leader will teach you that rules are the only constant. Universal laws cannot be bent.

Forgive everyone, no matter what, but always understand the lessons you learned with them. You can't do hurtful things to people and expect to live a peaceful life. Do not be afraid have the faith, courage, strength, and bravery to stand up for what you believe in, even if that means you have to stand alone.

Be aware when you are in alignment with your higher purpose. People in powerful authoritarian positions act above jurisdiction and laws, but trust that universal and Karmic laws must be enforced, balanced, and respected. Let them be wrong about you; there is nothing to prove.

As a leader, know that you have the power to change people's stars. Everything happens for a reason. It may not make sense right now, but give it time and it will. Everything that's tried to destroy me in my life, I have dealt with on my own. I cried myself to sleep, picked myself back up, and dried my own tears. I have grown from things that were meant to break me. I get stronger every day, and I have God to thank for that. Karma says that if you destroy someone's life with lies, slandering, or bullying, take it as a loan, because it is coming back to you with interest.

I will never forget who helped me during difficult times, who put me in difficult times, and who left me in difficult times. Keep your distance from people who will never admit that they were wrong. They will never admit their part in the wrongdoing for the attacking of innocent victims for the illusion of status, greed, money, clout, and power. Stop giving people power before you learn the facts. Before you judge, understand why. Before you before you hurt someone, before you speak, think. Karma says that everything you do will directly backfire on you.

Trust the journey; the hidden truth will be revealed soon enough, and you'll eventually figure it all out. It will make perfect sense: the players, planning, deceit, manipulation, treachery, lies, deception, betrayals, and corruption will be exposed.

Karma will play out in their own lives for the destruction they created in your lifetime. Karma and universal law cannot be broken and must be balanced. Judgement will be based upon the facts of what happened to you. Stop using your energy to worry, and learn to stay away from people you have already healed from. Protect your space; not everyone gets an invite. Use your energy to plant positive things, believe, create, love, grow, glow, manifest, and heal.

As soon as you remember the self-love journey and choose yourself, everything else falls in alignment. It's the season of Dharma when you choose yourself.

Leaders, the biggest thing I've learned this year is not to force anything, including conversations, friendships, relationships, opportunities, attention, and love. Anything forced is not worth fighting for. If it flows, it flows, and if it crashes, it crashes. It is what it is.

Green flags in leaders:

- They celebrate your wins and will not trip you up at the finish line.
- They remember the small things about you.
- They respect your boundaries.

- You feel energized around them.
- They listen without being defensive.
- They allow you to fully be yourself.
- They make you feel safe and protected.
- You do not have to watch what you say.
- They support your goals.
- They have the vision to lead you down the correct yellow brick road and path.

When you put all your time and energy into attacking innocent people, the wrongdoings and deeds you did to others without regret do carry penalties. Earning a spot, position, title, or status by participating in a community, company, team, religion, cult, secret society, mean girls who were paid to bully, abuse, vengeance, lies, treason, bigotry, blasphemy, spite, hate, causing harm, winning at all costs, financial gain, deception, entitlement, cheating, competition, chaos, harassment, ego, stalking, greed, committing power plays, blocking relationships/work opportunities, gossip, slander, biases, stealing and selling your souls for attacking innocent individuals for profit is against humanity, universal, and judicial laws These are punishable crimes committed against humanity and innocent people, and they are not tolerated.

Leaders know they must be willing to choose the path of resistance. No one could ever walk one hour or one day in my shoes or path and know the self-love healing journey I chose to endure to be here today. Do not get discouraged; give yourself permission to walk away and disconnect from toxic people, betrayals, haters, destructive frenemies, and damaged relationships that you have outgrown or which no longer serve your higher purpose. Thank them for crossing your path and for the opportunity to learn the lessons.

You are your own superhero. Every day is a blessing and is the real deal. Holyfield—you can never compete where you don't compare. I have survived through things meant to break me. I cried myself to sleep, picked myself back up, and dried my own tears. I am ready for the next chapter of my life. I choose to be a survivor, not a victim.

Guilt—one little lie, no one's going to know, one little lie to avoid the smoke and fire of secrets, clout, greed, money, power, and status. They collaborated and threw you under the bus to hide their wrongdoings, ghosting before telling the truth. Their secrets are exposed.

One little lie...no one's going to know the destruction caused by this group without remorse or regret. One little lie...no one's going to know how much the lies, slander, defamation, and bullying destroyed an innocent person. The truth is that they do not want anyone to know the horrible mistake they made when they collaborated to harm and betray an innocent person.

Leaders choose the higher ground and rise like a phoenix out of the ashes. They choose the path of love and forgiveness despite the chaos, lies, threats, thievery, deceit, harassment, bullying, hatred, jealousy, envy, and blocking of opportunities for the lifestyles of greed, status, and glamour. Leaders choose to be a survivor, not a victim.

A leader will fly like an eagle and has the vision to guide people through the journey. Leaders, sometimes we must detach from what we wanted for ourselves or what we have outgrown to get to what we actually deserve. Give love to whatever gives you love, show up for yourself, and refuse to quit; it's not an option. No matter what, I choose to be a survivor not a victim.

As leaders, we can negatively influence the culture of the workplace environment when we refuse to acknowledge that respect is the glue that holds companies together. You become what you surround yourself with, Energy is contagious, so choose wisely your environment. It can impact your life.

Martin Luther King fought for world peace and was motivated to protect our communities from any injustices. He believed that any biases, bigotry, hatred, harassment, and violence against religious beliefs, gender, and race is an injustice, and an injustice against anyone is a threat to justice everywhere. Protect our communities and report biases, bigotry, based hatred, and harassment crimes.

We can't always have a good day, but we make a conscious decision to get up, show up, choose our attitudes, and make good choices. I would say to my children every day before they left for school, "We all have access to the three C's in life: choices, chances, and change." I choose to be a survivor, not a victim of my life. I choose to forgive and not to invite chaos in my life.

Leadership is not about you; it's about helping to inspire and facilitate the success of others. Let them be upset when you picked peace over drama and distance over disrespect.

Having a leader with a good heart and positive energy is a blessing. It wasn't luck that got you this far! Consequences must be balanced, so before you react, think about it: every behavior, decision you make or do not make, and action has consequences. You cannot save anyone from their own mistakes and actions.

Sometimes the best way to add to your life is just subtract from it. Release yourself from toxic situations, connections, and relationships. These actions do have consequences. Every loss isn't a loss. Behind every strong person, there is a story that gave them no choice but to survive the bullying, harassment, stalking, hatred, suffering, sadness, depression, painful memories, desperation, betrayals, and hidden truths. There are people who may be upset because you healed and you picked peace over drama and distance over disrespect.

Don't judge my breakthrough until you know what I survived and have been through. Everything is unfolding in divine timing, and the history of unfortunate events can never be eradicated, erased, or forgotten. You get tested the most when it's time to elevate. Don't break—remember, pressure makes diamonds, and you alchemized this betrayal into an empire.

Leadership begins when you combine love of humanity, integrity, honesty, truth, and respect. You can't live your life for other people; you have to do what's right for you, even if it hurts someone else.

How you treat others when no one is looking is your integrity and the hallmark standard of authenticity. Instead of protecting world peace and humanity and fighting for freedom, we follow the principles, values, and loyalty to corruption, criminal justice, money, greed, bribery, arrogance of government power, misuse of public funds, and conspiracy. We hide abuse, allow violations of illegal use of surveillance, wrongdoings of religious faiths, secret societies, cults, churches, worship groups, criminal organizations, criminal gangs, and political corruption.

Be the culture that stands out and cares more about living in truth, honesty, principles, humanity, and integrity. One person who has integrity can change the world.

Leaders never forget that it takes courage and strength to push through all the hard times. They were not sorry when YOU didn't know the truth about the lies, bullying, false reporting, stalking, false accusations, slander, levels of deceit, defamation, and lack of evidence and empathy that they participated in to ruin your life. Remember that.

"Better a poor man who walks in his integrity and truth than a rich man, crooked in his ways."

Be honest; they may not like the real truth, but at least it's the truth. There's no need to cut people off; just grow, and they will eventually fall off. No matter what you do, someone will always talk about you and question your judgment. Just make choices that you can live with.

Leaders never forget that it takes courage and strength to push through all the hard times. They were not sorry when YOU didn't know the truth about the lies, bullying, false reporting, stalking, false accusations, slander, levels of deceit, defamation, lack of evidence and empathy they participated in to ruin your life- remember that.

"Better a poor man who walks and his integrity and truth than a rich man, crooked and his ways."

Be honest, they may not like the real truth but at least it's the truth. No need to cut people off just grow they will eventually fall off. No matter what you do, someone will always talk about you and question your judgment, just make choices that you can live with.

I trust the next chapter and story of my life, because I am the author. Respect yourself enough to just walk away from people and things that no longer serve your higher purpose. Stop seeking forgiveness from people who can't even be honest with themselves. Your doubts are liars. Your fears are thieves. Don't trust the lies they tell. The forgiveness is for you to heal and move forward.

Everyone has a Bible verse. Mine is Proverbs 3.5–6. Trust in God with all your heart, and don't lean on your own understanding. In all ways, acknowledge him, and he will direct your paths. Let go and trust with all your heart in the divine journey! I think we believe we are the drivers of our destiny, but this proves who the driver is who directs your path and how you really didn't have control at all.

The time is always right; never regret being a good person to the wrong people. The courage it takes to leave behind what's not for you and what you have outgrown or what doesn't fit your narrative anymore is the same courage that will help you find your way to your purpose, your destiny, and what is meant for you.

Remember, you cannot fix people who refuse to grow. Things bloom, thrive and grow where you water and tend them. Not allowing anyone to waste your time is another sign of self-love and respect. Move on and move forward like you never knew them, because the reality is, you didn't.

When people really love you, you know, because they don't talk about it; they act on it. When things are not in your best interest, don't give a response, action, or altercation; just don't feed it. That's where the true power lies. People who are your true friends would never believe in rumors or gossip.

It's during times of adversity and change that the true character and integrity of a leader is tested and revealed. How did you help humanity during times of upheaval? Did you cower and hide like an ostrich in the sand pretending nothing happened?

How did you demonstrate and navigate through when facing unexpected events in rapid changing environments? True leaders don't talk about it; they act on it. When people or things are not in your best interest no response, no action, no altercations, just don't feed it.

It's all about how you handled the flames. The steel of life's fiery trials will make you into a weapon for destruction or a tool for building. If you know my life story, then you know how I believe in the power of prayer. If they refuse to evolve, it is a them problem, not yours. Always get back up on your feet.

It's never too late to reinvent yourself and create new ideas. Be the change. Toxic people project their own character defects onto their team. They do this by accusing a person of the exact actions they themselves do...but deny. Pride and ego are concerned with who is right, and humility is concerned with what is right.

Never forget that it takes courage and strength to push through all the hard times. They were not sorry when YOU didn't know the truth about the lies, bullying, false reporting, stalking, false accusations, slander, levels of deceit, defamation, and lack of evidence and empathy that they participated in to ruin your life. Remember that.

"Better a poor man who walks in his integrity and truth than a rich man, crooked in his ways."

Be honest: they may not like the real truth, but at least it's the truth. There's need to cut people off; just grow, and they will eventually fall off. No matter what you do, someone will always talk about you and question your judgment, so you should just make choices that you can live with. You become unstoppable the moment you know how to convert pain into strength. People only rain on your parade because they are jealous of your sun and tired of their shade. EMPOWER EACH OTHER.

Some people can only talk about you because they lost the privilege to talk to you! These people are a reflection of your own readiness and determination to achieve growth. Together, you are walking each other home to authenticity and wholeness.

Once you carry your own water, you will learn the value of every drop. Have faith that we are always tested. Don't give up. The things you are hoping for will come at an unexpected time. This is divine timing.

People only try to ruin your sunlight because they are jealous of your sunlight. Just forgive them and let Karma handle them. Turn pain into power and sorrow into strength! Hurt people hurt people, and healed people heal people. Don't be triggered by their actions. It is their consequences and their judgment for the way they treated you.

Recently, I was thinking of the nine churches I have been baptized in. All the churches I attended had different versions of the Bible, false prophets, preachers, faiths, and beliefs which lead people down the wrong path. Where did they receive their training? Then, I had an epiphany: God has no religion.

He only requires prayer. During these days of global pandemic and uncertainty, may we pray for the protection, safety, and health of all humanity. May these prayers infuse our spirit with strength, hope, and fate, that together we may witness empowerment. It's never too late to reinvent yourself and create new ideas. Sometimes life puts us in a direct path to the very best time of our life. Enjoy the journey. Have the courage, determination, and bravery to move forward. Get back up on your feet.

People will always try to use the love you had for them against you. Turn pain into power. When you have set healthy boundaries, have faith that there is no more heartache for you! My mission is to continue to expose darkness. That's been my mission, my task, and my purpose.

Prayer is breathing in the sacred light of God. Feel with every inhale that you are at a higher vibration. Holy Spirit, we ask that you purify every soul, each tissue and organ, with the holy light of God. Holy Spirit, we ask you to walk before us as a teacher and as a friend, teaching us how to discern the evil and wickedness.

We call for the holy angels. Archangel Rafael, say the word and everything will be healed. Archangel Michael, please show us with your purple shield, clear us, and put us in a pillar of God's light. Shield us and activate God's pillar of light. With love to all and all to light, we call back our power on our past, present, and future timelines, and we are recalibrated to God's divine light and frequency of divine love.

We ask our Archangel Gabriel to help protect us on our journey. Lord Jesus, we ask that you rebuke and transmute any energy not of piece, love, and light and return it to God. From Archangel Uriel, we asked that you bring us forward into our divine love and light. From Archangel Metatron, please, we are protected on all six planes of consciousness, as above, so below. We hold space, believe in miracles, and pray our world leaders hear the voice of God to make the right decisions. We pray for anyone who is prosecuted right now, anyone who needs a home, shelter, food, job, or car, anyone struggling who needs a miracle for addictions or poor health. We hold space for a miracle. If the Lord Jesus gave you the ability to give miracles, where would you hold this miracle? Would you hold it for yourself or for someone across the world who may need food today? Holding the vibration of a miracle worker, inhale, exhale, and pray for a higher frequency and vibration of love with God. All is possible in love in and in archangels. We welcome you!

We work for God, and the only one who can fire us is him and no one else. Stand in your love and light. God fights your battles; surrender, and he will give you back what you lost. Our abundance comes from God, the spirit, and the universe. Speak your truth and shine your light; it connects you to God's consciousness. The reason we're here in this world is to express a high vibration of consciousness and holy love. The more you are in truth, the more God's light shines on you. Speak and walk in your truth and express and vibrate at higher love.

I understand that this is the matrix, and there's a higher purpose. It's up to our soul to seize growth opportunities. You can choose not to awaken, but you're never guaranteed another life cycle or opportunity to heal. Close out all Karmic cycles, ask for forgiveness, and pray for protection for your energy.

We all make mistakes, regret decisions and poor choices, and choose the wrong paths. Remember that the people who hold jealousy, fear, resentment, contempt, confusion, crisis, chaos, cheating, falsehoods, revenge, hatred, secret society pacts, competition, wars, deceitful behavior, toxicity, corruption, and envy for any person are misaligned.

The best apology is changed behavior. Make decisions based on what should happen, not what shouldn't. The world is made of faith and trust and a little pixie dust.

You make decisions based upon your own personal beliefs, experiences, ideas, uses, intuition, visions, experiences, ethics, values, and convictions. If your actions inspire people to do more, dream more, and become more, you are a leader.

Be careful of the vitriol, stealthy lies, persecution, and maniacal bullies acting as though they were innocent of their atrocities when the truth of their motives was revealed. They will try to manipulate your actions into believing they have nothing to do with the situation.

It reminds me of Kaa in *The Jungle Book* hiding the fact he is a snake who hypnotiz's the victim to never think about the consequences of their crimes and behaviors

Sometimes people don't hate you for the things you have. Sometimes they harbor envy, jealousy, and hatred towards you because you can go through life's worst enemies, horrific moments, difficult times, and life-changing experiences and still hold your head up high and come out on top—all while looking like you never went through anything in your life.

Faith does not mean that trusting God will shield and protect us from the lessons of Karma or from the storms we created. It means trusting him to make us strong enough to walk through the storms. Some storms are here to clear the path.

We all have consequences for our actions: it's Karma, universal judgement, and civil rights. When we focus on our purpose and invest our energy into visions, positivity, and creativity rather than drama, there is no time for negativity.

Gratitude is the magnet used to manifest miracles. Visualize yourself as your highest self and show up as that person. You don't always get to choose what you go through in life, but you have to choose to grow through what you go through. Remember, to struggle is strength.

Recently, I received an alert from Facebook notifying me there was access to my personal pictures and files for the last six months. The alert said I had the option to allow or limit the access. Despite having the new iPhone, I noticed it had not performed properly for the past few years. After I received the alert, I contacted Apple IT and AT&T Tech support. Apple identified several problems with tracking apps, surveillance devices, viruses, and data corruption. Apple confirmed my iPhone was hacked, tracked, blocked, and uploaded with surveillance tracking software, and they found two unknown devices.

My iPhone failed to charge, was extremely hot when charging, cellular data usage was high, the system randomly switched on at night, hotspot usage ran down same day, I had not received inbound calls, emails, or texts, the phone ringer was turned off, Siri was turned off, and there was extremely slow performance when using the cellular data.

This year, I received a barrage of breach of personal information mail, including requests to change passwords, verify emails, and click on corrupted website links. Concerned about my privacy being violated, I had Apple support validate thousands of electronic applications created in Linkedin, Glassdoor, Indeed, and company and recruitment sites that vanished without a trace or a response.

This was shocking. After two hours Apple located everything in the loud, and it's clear it can never be erased. There is always a permanent footprint. If I ask about it, I know about it. So don't lie about it.

Never believe you're above anyone else. Embrace humility, be humble, protect integrity, respect honesty, and be grateful. Ideally, if you choose to participate in lies, jealousy, biases, bigotry, gossip, and rumors about anyone else, you cannot act with pious hypocrisy and hide behind religion as principled and divinely guided. Hate is hate, and Karma must be balanced.

Focus on continuously improving yourself by improving your performance, self-confidence, vision, values, trust, integrity, and positive relationships with others. Good leadership will always follow the laws, and if they made mistakes they will act responsibly, while poor leadership will always lead people down the wrong paths and will lead them to find a way around the laws.

> "Justice has nothing to do with what goes on in the courtroom; Justice is what comes out of a courtroom."
> —Clarence Darr

We all have consequences for our actions: it's Karma, universal judgement, and civil rights. When we focus on our purpose and invest our energy into visions, positivity, and creativity rather than drama, there is no time for negativity.

Gratitude is the magnet to manifest miracles. Visualize yourself in your highest self, and show up as that person. You don't always get to choose what you go through in life, but you have to choose to grow through what you go through. Remember, to struggle is strength.

The truth always wins! Do not hide behind false narratives, lies, fraudulent statements, false accusations, or fake information, and don't hide from your mistakes, because the truth is always exposed. You had the courage to close the door behind you, and it only made you stronger.

Sometimes in the moment we cannot understand or comprehend the atrocities and the terrible actions of others, but God will put you back together right in front of the people who broke you. Karma is living your best life. Give yourself permission to move forward in a new life.

I'm so proud of my children, who have made it through the most impossible dark times with dignity, kindness, respect, and love. Thank goodness for the amazing people you have become; you are an example to others.

When you participated in corruption, spread lies, laughed about having the power of status/title to ruin people's lives, careers, reputations, opportunities, blocked communication, theft, stalking, bullying, perjury, privacy violations, contracts, or knowingly caused conscious damage and destruction of innocent people, the infliction is irreversible.

We all have choices. If you chose to cause harm, pain, or suffering, the consequence is Karma. The truth of hidden actions, agendas, religions, bigotry, politics, secret relationships, vows, pacts, promises, and publicly casting illusions will be revealed. Balance is being restored in your life as the Karmic lessons of how they participated and paid money to cause broken illusions.

Trust me, when you are good to people, it circles back to you. Helping others in humanity by spreading love, compassion, and kindness of your heart is your greatest strength and purpose. This will earn you good Karma points.

However, if you continue to hide behind the fact that your true hatred caused unjust war, cruelty, lies, deception, brutality, bribery, theft, greed, deceit, intimidation tactics, secret society corruption, criminal actions, harm, revenge, retaliation, loss of job opportunities, harassment, or abuse of power and destruction, this stems from an exposed mindset of your own religious beliefs, immorality, false narratives, immaturity, obsessive mental health issues, addictions, and own personal belief systems. These are your choices, down to toxic lifestyles, values, and affairs.

Instead of leading others, focus on your personal journey, self-love, self-improvement, gratitude for the blessings, inspiring others towards a higher purpose, giving love to others, healing, and learning from past mistakes. you chose to avoid your growth. If you don't focus on these things, you've wasted valuable energy, effort, and time trying convince a community you were innocent of any wrongdoings.

You cannot reverse Karma. Every action is recorded in the Akashic library and reviewed by the universal court to ensure accountability and accuracy of righteous judgement. Everyone has their own path, choices, and consequences. This applies to anyone who participated to help cover up the lies of intentional deception to cause harm because they did not want the truth to be revealed and exposed. Karma will be balanced. Where did you plant your own seeds?

Another day of opportunity is in front of you, so you can live your best life. We are all tested on our journey to make sure we learned the lessons. Remember to forgive them for your healing. It does not mean that you allow them into your life. You forgave and prayed for them from afar. How you were treated is their Karma, how you treat them is yours. Unless you focus on healing, loving yourself, practicing forgiveness, and eliminating toxic relationships no longer in alignment with your higher purpose, you can never elevate.

Before crossing someone, you'd better gain knowledge about their spiritual rank and level. You do not want a relationship with someone who is a low vibrational person experiencing a lot of negative Karma, losses, hatred, arrogance, arguments, narcissistic tendencies, bad luck, and drama. It's not your job to heal, save, or change them—let them go. That's why every day is valuable, because you are never guaranteed another day.

Think about energy as a lifetime magnet. You do not want to attract other people's burdens and negative Karmic lessons after you've already healed yourself, elevated yourself, and learned the lessons. Some people end up messing up just by being dirty, lying, and deceitful!

Pour into the lives that pour equally into yours. In order to heal, you must hurt; in order to love, you must break; in order to have peace, you must face chaos. Never regret any experience in your life, because it is always meant to bring you balance. Set firm boundaries and protect your peace. Do not allow people from your past to sabotage your life after you've already learned the lesson.

Trust in the universe that all illusions are broken. Let Karma be the wrecking ball to seek your justice. Righteous judgment is called on a community that hid behind their own outrageous involvement in years of treachery, secret society, misuse of power, bribery, religious persecution, bigotry, biases, perjury, dishonesty, greed, deception, online stalking, threats, illegal businesses, illegal phone hacking/surveillance, shadow banning, allegations, defamation of employer, financial ruin, unfair/unjust dismissal, purposely blocking access to opportunities, illegal falsified statements/reports/faxes/calls/texts/emails/letters, thousands of false accusations made to employers, leaking personal data, identity theft, judicial crimes, affairs, slander, addictions, propaganda, traitors, betrayal, bullying, lying, cheating, harassment, and hatred against an innocent person and their family. It's all fun and games until the truth, testimony, and evidence are revealed.

Be Grateful You Are Not the Gatekeepers

It does not matter what status you hold if your actions were taken for clout, power, greed, ranking, or title. You cannot take shortcuts in life. The fact is, you lacked the leadership, vision, capacity, intelligence, and knowledge and cast illusions, defamation, slander, insults, criticisms, and lies to hide behind the plagiarism of someone else's ideas and lifetime achievement. Theft is against corporate ethics, civil laws, and universal principles. Karma must be balanced.

In truth, all illusion is broken. Let Karma be your wrecking ball. You cannot hide from the facts.

Everyone wants your spot until they find out what it takes to play the position. The hardest thing to do is grieve for a person when they are still alive. They do not know about the burdens, struggles, challenges, roadblocks, and boulders thrown on my path. I used them to build my own empire.

Behind every strong person, there is a story that gave them only two options: to sink or swim. I chose to swim the marathon. The storms will only make you a stronger swimmer.

Positive people are not positive because they've skated through life. They're positive because they've been through hell and decided not to live there anymore. I had to learn the difference between who was in my corner and who was in my business.

Depending upon the circumstances, sometimes our lives have to be completely changed, broken down, destroyed, shaken up, and rearranged to get us on the right path. Unfortunately, we cannot intercede when Karmic, universal, constitutional rights, and judiciary laws were violated. Judgement is the same, and consequences will have to be imposed.

That move you're hesitant to make could be the one that positively changes your life forever. Despite the struggles, I'll always choose to share the most genuine love I can offer. May happiness fill you and heal you.

You all know without hesitation a person who practices self-love, performs acts of altruism, leadership, love for humanity, leads people from their heart, has healing spirit, kindness, compassion, inspiration, love, light, and insight to guide humanity comes from the most high God. Many of you wear masks and hold counterfeit faith and belief systems. You joined forces to attack and persecute the innocent on God's mission to help guide humanity, practice peace, forgiveness, love, and healing. Do you live in God's truth?

So we are clear, when you practice destruction, lies, greed, manipulation, illusion, corruption, theft, hatred, harm, commit perjury, slander, bullying, harassment, illegal activities, dishonesty, and conspiracy, you are fraudulent and do not hold power over anyone. That is the delusional belief of an enemy who practices dishonesty and corruption and is a mental psychopath, stalker obsessed lunatic, psychotic copycat, and doppelgänger. Definitely not God made. You reap what you sow, and you cannot hide from Karma. It must be balanced.

You are not a victim of their actions, poor leadership, and management styles. The key is to hold the power and to be accountable for yourself and how others affect you. Stay strong, stand in your own power, set boundaries, and take control of your own mind, body, and soul. I declare that I am strong and healed. Simply choose to open a new door and close the doors of the past behind you. Remember, you have many opportunities and choices in this lifetime. Take the leap of faith in the new direction.

Let them live in the illusions, judging, lying, stalking, bullying, harassment, hatred, stealing, gossiping, and outrageous allegations because you knew their real skeletons in the closet. Instead, you chose the path to cherish, honor, respect, dignity, authenticity, values, soulful connections, compassion, happiness, harmony, and building connections.

Your legacy is to focus on yourself, be a good person of morality and a humanitarian leader who builds trust and practices compassion, kindness, respect, and integrity. People will believe how resilient you are when you hold yourself accountable to integrity, believe in yourself, and practice confidence, self-love, admiration, and respect.

They will inevitably inherit absolutely nothing, wasting energy and valuable time on greediness, envy, revenge, gluttony, addictions, corruption, contempt, obstruction, obsession, and jealousy. If you do not show forgiveness, none will be shown to you. Let it go, allow Karma to backfire, and be the judge in your life.

You are not a victim of their actions and poor leadership and management styles. The key is with you. You hold the power to be accountable for yourself and how others affect you. Stay strong, stand in your own power, set boundaries, and take control of your own mind, body, and soul. I declare that I am strong and healed. Simply choose to open a new door and close the doors of the past behind you. Remember, you have many opportunities and choices in this lifetime. Take the leap of faith in the new direction.

It literally does not matter what other people think, as long as you know the truth. Pour into your own cup, assuming your cup is full and overflowing. What belongs in your cup is for you.

Believe that your higher self is being divinely guided to make the right decisions in all areas of your life as it pertains to divine relationships and as it relates to finances and every aspect of your life, so be it. If you do not show forgiveness, none will be shown to you. Let it go and allow Karma to backfire and be the judge in your life.

What is a legacy you will leave behind? If you learn from the universe, then you know your worth. The blessings you receive are because of the hard work, strength, your resilience, and your determination that you will leave a legacy of love. Their reality is not your reality. Let them live their life. Let them talk about you and gossip about you. You live your life and worry about your path and journey. What is your legacy you're going to leave behind for generations?

The thing about me is that I will never hate anyone. The truth of how you treat me will never change me. I will fall back and learn to deal with you differently and love you from a distance. What I won't do is reciprocate bad energy. I'll just love you and wish you the best, but I choose to no longer be part of your circle.

Your BELIEFS, outdated views, religious dogma, and political ideology don't make you a good person...your faith, helping humanity, behavior, and actions do. No matter how dark things seem to get, never give up. Keep going, you've got this. Believe that.

We are all going through a difficult time. I hope we can all find peace. It takes a lot of strength to choose solitude over being around negative or toxic people. Be grateful and live like every day is a blessing.

- I am not sick.
- I have clothes to wear.
- I have running water.
- I have food to eat.
- Life is good.
- I am thankful to God.

It doesn't matter what immoral behaviors and toxicity you tolerated in the past; you learned from the lessons, healed, and moved on. Whenever you choose to close the doors that led you down the wrong direction and open the new doors to opportunity, you start attracting amazing people and everything else meant for you.

People are always going to talk about you no matter what, so do whatever makes you happy. You deserve joy. When I look back one year from now, I am going to say, "Damn, I really did believe and had faith in myself, and it worked!"

When you have a heart of gold and pure intentions, you don't lose anyone, they lose you.

Nobody watches you harder than the people who don't like you. These are jealous, envious, hateful people, so give them a show they will never forget.

Cut toxic people off and letting them live with whatever lies, misinformation and delusional story they've come up with. Some people are going to reject you because you shine too bright for them. You are the best upgrade you'll ever work on. Restart. Reset. Refocus as many times as you need to. Just don't ever give up on yourself.

I don't seek revenge; the fact that you no longer have access is enough. I am proud of person I was in the past. The struggles, the difficulty, and the challenges shake me into the person I am today. She looked at her old life one last time and whispered, "I am ready. It's time for my new future to begin."

Today, I met a girl who's gone to hell and back her whole life, and she made it. She looked back at her old life one last time, inhaled deeply, and whispered to herself, "It is time. I am ready for my new story to begin."

You become your best self when you work on things that people can't take away from you. Have a mindset of character, integrity, innovation, authenticity, grit, discipline, honesty, and kindness. You glow differently when you mind your business, work hard in silence, stay in prayer, and keep your circle small.

Insecure people seek revenge. Strong people forgive and let go. Smart people ignore the behaviors focused on pettiness, failure to disclose, lies, secrets, slander, duplicity, toxicity, malice, hatred, contempt, stealing, criticism, cruelty, defamation, bullying, falsifying evidence, masking, plagiarism, blocking communications, jealousy, and obsession.

The most wonderful moment in a person's life is when you realize you can do whatever you want, you don't owe anyone an explanation, and you don't need anyone's permission. Have the courage, determination, and bravery to move forward.

We survived too many storms to be bothered by a few raindrops. Shift your mindset from 'I don't know if I can' to 'I will figure it out.' Believe and have faith. Even if they try to take everything away from you, YOU will just take a pause, adjust the crown, and go get it all over again. Remember, it's not on me, it's within me. You are in control of your own destiny.

Silence is the new answer to disrespect. You choose to no longer react, to no longer argue, to no longer dive into the drama. You simply remove your presence. Can you relate? People ask me, "Why is it so hard to trust people?" The real question is, "Why is it so hard for people to tell the truth?"

When someone is under the illusion that they have had power and authority to do you wrong and they don't believe in Dharma/Karma or the truth that you know you are divinely guided and protected by angels, spirit guides, the universe, God, and source energy, that's a them problem, not a you problem.

Strong people never give up; we take a break and come back stronger than ever. We don't have time to be petty, jealous, or envious, because we are too busy counting our blessings and are still clapping when someone else is a winner. You can't bring down a person who learned to walk alone. Even when we fall, we get right back up again, dust ourselves off, and come back even stronger to win the race.

Life is too short, and you'll never get the same little moments and time again, so don't waste it. Things will change, but life goes on! You are not a victim anymore, and you are not the product of your circumstances, but you are the product of your own actions, failures, and decisions, which do have consequences.

Some people will judge you for changing. Others will celebrate you for growing. Choose your circle wisely. Put your happiness first. It starts with you. You will never know how long we have, so remind yourself that life is for living. Gift yourself peace, love, enjoyment, and forgiveness,

I'm loving this version of myself. I know to set boundaries and take a stand for myself, and I am the kind of person who understands her worth without apologizing for who she is.

I love that I don't care anymore—not in a hurtful way, but in a peaceful way. The older you get, the more you realize that the real luxuries in life are time, slow mornings, and the freedom of choice.

Remember to be humble enough to know that you can be replaced and wise enough to know that there is nobody else like you. That moment when you have found your people who will match your energy and encourage you to be bold is the moment you see yourself in all your glory!

It's crazy how the more you love yourself, the more you detach from things that don't love you. Don't quit. Sometimes the things you are hoping for come at unexpected times.

People will hate you, rate you, gossip, shake you, and break you, but how strong you stand is what makes you. Sometimes you just have to be done—not mad, not upset, not angry, not jealous, not envious, not making excuses, no being sad, not blaming, not regretting or seeking revenge. Just be done.

Be proud of yourself for dealing with the truth, healing from the pain of past trauma, and struggling with life's worst days of desperation, darkness, and suffering. You always see the light at the end of every tunnel. Follow your path, believe in faith, and hope that there is a rainbow at the end of every storm.

Pay attention to whom your energy increases and decreases around, because that's the universe giving you a hint of who you should embrace or stay away from. Let Karma be the catalyst for their judgements—not because life has been easy, perfect, and exactly as you anticipated, but because you chose to be happy and grateful for all the blessings you have received. Let go of what's gone, be grateful for what remains, and look forward to what is coming next.

Remember Who You Are and Why You're Here

You're never given anything in this world that you can't handle. Be strong, be kind, be flexible, love yourself, and love others. Always remember to just keep moving forward.

You are the driver of your own life. Don't let anyone else steal your seat or path. Do not waste time thinking about what you could have done differently. TRUST that when it's gone, it's gone.

1. "A false witness will not go unpunished, and whoever pours out lies will perish." (Proverbs 19:9)
2. "No one who practices deceit will dwell in my house; no one who speaks falsely will stand in my presence." (Psalm 101:7)
3. "An honest witness does not deceive, but a false witness pours out lies." (Proverbs 14:5)

Trust is like a glass; once broken, it will never be the same again. In the end, you'll know who's fake, who's true, and who will risk it all for you. I don't get mad anymore. I just accept it for what it is and move on.

A strong woman didn't become strong overnight. She became strong by overcoming all the things that were meant to destroy her. Judge me by the people I avoid. Be strong, be flexible, love yourself, and love others. Always remember, just keep moving forward.

Self-love—when you love yourself, you glow from the inside. You attract people who respect and appreciate your energy. Everything starts with how you feel about yourself. Start feeling worthy, valuable, and deserving of receiving the best life has to offer. Be magnetic.

They cursed your name privately, But GOD WIII BLESS YOUR LIFE PUBLICLY! People don't want to hear this, but words not matching actions is called manipulation, and refusing to be held accountable for it is called gaslighting. We're talking abuse.

When life gives you lemons, trust in God to make lemonade. These same people who have publicly targeted me for years wanted to make themselves feel more powerful by telling people lies and slander, harassing me, and bullying me to ruin my life. This hate group caused me stress by blocking every single work opportunity, communication, and contact, and falsely accusing me of poor work ethics, unacceptable behavior, and misconduct.

This was a game they played to win at all costs—my cost, my reputation, my ability, my talent, my skills, my life, and my work. They sent threats and paid people in organizations, companies, secret societies, and religious communities to cause conflict with bonuses. The reality is a group of jealous, insecure haters who targeted me to cause me harm for no reason. I am innocent, but everyone else was paid a bribe to break me, cause me trouble and conflicts, and harm me and my life. The truth hurts, and I know it was colleagues. I know about the insecure behavior.

They are projecting their own character flaws, biases, lies jealousy, envy, hate, and toxic behaviors. The reality is that they are just mirroring themselves and projecting onto me.

She is in her own lane, and there's no speed limit or traffic to slow her down! Pray, focus manifest, and let go of the negative energy or anything that's going to slow you down.

Know your worth. Anything that does not value you, your presence, or your efforts should simply be removed. Happy people are not happier because they have everything in life. It is because they have developed the ability to see the good in the things that happen to them.

God has removed you from a table where you used to sit in order to save you from a host who was serving you poison. You are not broken. You are healed, healthy, and whole. Let that sink in.

Your boundaries are not making you lose friends or family members. Your boundaries are making you lose gaslighters, emotional abusers, needy and greedy manipulators, self-centered narcissists, and energy-draining vampires. Keep standing up for yourself. You're doing great, so keep going. Surround yourself with people who push you to be better. No drama, jealousy, or mess, just higher goals, good vibes, and positive energy. Pray, focus, manifest, and let go of the negative energy or anything that's going to slow you down.

Nobody will apologize for how they treat you, but they surely will blame you for the way you react. No matter how much I like someone, the moment they make me question my worth and act inconsistently, I'm done. My self-love, respect, dignity, and determination are bigger than my feelings.

You can't bring down a person who isn't afraid to eat alone, set boundaries, or lose friends, who doesn't care about rejection and who doesn't tolerate disrespect. When you profoundly hurt someone deeply, act blinded from the truth, blameless for these actions, playing a victim, you created the cruelty, misery, suffering, havoc, pain, lies, destruction, damage, and betrayals. These are forms of immaturity, psychopathic behavior, and mental illness.

When you forgive, you do not erase the memory. You simply choose to forgive, to free yourself from the bitterness. The memory stays not to be forgotten, but to be remembered as a valuable lesson. When our time here on earth is done, money or material things will not matter, but the love, time, and kindness we've given others will shine and live on forever.

Be fearless; sometimes the bad things that happen in our lives are meant to happen and to redirect us back towards the path. They may be the best things that will ever happen to us. I am a firm believer in what's meant to be, will be. If something doesn't work out, it simply wasn't meant for you, and there's something better on the way.

Notice how people change when they don't get what they want from you. Remember: you are the heroine in your own story.

You no longer fear the flames because you became the fire. No one has a bigger comeback than someone who's been burned by learning they can't count on the ones that they trusted with their whole heart. Don't be afraid to be alone; the sun is alone every day and still shines.

It doesn't matter how dirty others play. Karma has a big appetite these days. Shift your mindset towards thinking, why do I allow people to treat me like that? To, why do I allow people in my space to mistreat me?

You have the power to rise up from anything.
You can completely reinvent yourself.
Everything is possible and temporary.
You're not stuck.
You have choices.
You can think new thoughts.

You can learn something new.
You can create new habits.

All that matters is that you decide today to never look back. Truth always comes out to support the narrative. Where is their proof to support the lies?

Strong women become strong by overcoming all the things that were meant to destroy them. Judge me by the people I avoid. Be strong, be flexible, love yourself, and love others. Always remember, just keep moving forward.

Self-Love—when you love yourself, you glow from the inside. You attract people who respect and appreciate your energy. Everything starts with how you see yourself. Start feeling worthy and deserving of receiving the best life has to offer. Be magnetic.

Trust is the key to any successful business and relationships. Worry about your character, not your reputation. Your character is who you are. Your reputation is who people think you are. You're not grown until you know how to communicate, apologize, be truthful, and accept accountability without blaming someone else.

Your next chapter is going to cause some people to wish they had treated you better. Friendship is not about who acts true to your face. It's about people who remain true behind your back. Self-love is the new relationship status.

Today's message—the butterfly is proof that you can go through a great deal of darkness and still become something beautiful. You don't just wake up and become the butterfly. Growth is a process.

The only people who deserve to be in your life are the ones who treat you with, love, kindness, and respect. You're about to overcome something you've been dealing with, and your mind and heart will soon be at peace again. None of us really know how much someone else is hurting. We could be standing right beside someone who feels completely broken or is facing the battle of their lives and have no idea. Be kind always.

Just keep swimming; no matter what's going on, keep on going. The truth is, it hurts her more than you will ever know. When she feels like she's going to fail, she keeps going; when she's tired, she keeps going. She knows standing still is not going to lead her to the life she deserves. You really think she's going to keep going, because it doesn't hurt her. She keeps going and will never look back. You can either be with her or get out of her way, because no matter what, she's going to keep on going.

The biggest life lesson is that we are not always in control. Life is full of experiences, lessons, heartbreak, and pain. It has also shown me love, compassion, kindness, hope, humility, beauty, positivity, positivity, peace, and New Beginnings.

Embrace it all. It makes us who we are, and after every storm comes a clear sky.

As you get older, you start to understand the difference between friends and associates, family and blood, business and work, love and lust, want and need. And most of all, you start to understand what's important, what's urgent, and what's not.

Sometimes we hold onto people more than they deserve because we focus on "how we felt before" instead of "how we suffer now." Don't kill people with kindness, because not everyone deserves your kindness. Kill people with silence, because not everyone deserves your attention.

You can't tame a strong soul on their journey. You might be a little bruised with permanent scars, but you will always refuse to be defeated. I wish only Karma for the people who treated me wrongly, and I am praying for them to remain calm, strong, humble, compassionate, respectful, loving, kind, and courageous whenever reality slaps them in the face.

Remember, I saved my reputation by knowing the entire truth and not telling anyone my personal story. You thought I would be fragile like a flower, but I chose to be fragile like a bomb. I was courageous when you thought I failed, but I stumbled and survived the destruction.

There is nothing stronger than a broken person who has rebuilt themselves. Do not let someone else who's never walked in your shoes tell you how to tie your shoes. Choose you, because when you start choosing you, you start attracting everything that is also choosing you.

A strong person didn't become strong overnight. They became strong by overcoming all the difficulties, challenges, and obstacles thrown at them that were meant to destroy them. Find something you are passionate about, believe it, get up every day, and fight. You are never guaranteed anything, so be grateful for having another day.

Life is about having loyalty, trust, and love. I'm celebrating myself loudly this year, and I don't care if nobody claps. I'll clap, really loud.

Was she always toxic, or only when her heart and trust was broken from the betrayals and lies? Remember, every single word, truth, lie, fact, and actions is reciprocated, documented, recorded, and communicated to ensure proper Karma is served.

The evidence is compared to laws violated in federal, criminal, universal, spiritual, and judicial justice. The facts are compared with the evidence presented against the accusations, statements made against those involved and proven to ensure accountability and accurate judgement. The reality is that nothing can change the outcome, and no one can really gets away with anything.

If you don't know the value of loyalty, you'll never understand the damage of betrayal. Everybody wants to be in your shoes until they see the work it takes to be in your position. Your taste in people changed once you started loving yourself. Stop wondering if you're good enough for them and start wondering if they're good for you. Keep moving forward!

"Red flags aren't always about the other person. When you start lying to yourself about who they are so that you don't have to face losing them, that's the flag to pay attention to." —Jillian Turecki

The wrong person will distract you, but the right one will motivate you to reach your full potential. Nothing is permanent. Don't stress yourself out too much, because no matter how bad the situation is, it will change.

Never forget how far you've come, everything you have gotten through, all the times you have pushed on even when you felt you couldn't. All the mornings you got out of bed no matter how hard it was. All the times you wanted to give up but you got through another day. Never forget how much strength you have developed along the way.

My major strength is that I lose interest in those who fail to recognize my value, and I'm completely unbothered by it; I simply remove my presence and move on. Don't be sad that people talk about you behind your back. They're in the right place...BEHIND YOU.

You're hoping I fall down, but I'm praying you get on your feet. We are not the same. She's not crazy, she was abused. She's not stupid, she was manipulated. She's not shy, she's protecting herself. She's not bitter, she's speaking the truth. She's not hanging onto the past, she's been damaged. She's not delusional, she lived a nightmare. She's not weak, she was trusting. She's not giving up, she's healing...

Are you strong enough to take the hits? The world is not all sunshine and rainbows. Life will beat you to your knees. It's about how hard you can take the hits. You are not a coward who points fingers and blames others. You are better than that!!!

When people repeatedly and intentionally undermine your character, integrity, and self-worth, just walk away. How many more chances, how many more times do you allow them to disrespect you? You learned your lessons; walk away. Enough is enough.

Some days are better, some days are worse. Look for the blessings instead of the curse. Be positive, stay strong. A secret to happiness is letting every situation be what it is instead of what you think it should be and then making the best of it.

Shift gears by changing lanes while dodging the obstructions, rocks, boulders, and potholes created by hateful rhetoric. Remember, obstacles in a mirror seem closer than they appear. I'm the same girl with the same name. I just have a different mindset and a new game.

Sometimes God removes people and things from your life because...

- He sees everything you don't.
- He hears everything you can't.
- He makes moves you won't.
- Trust Him with your entire life.

Use the haters as motivation. Never hate jealous, envious people. People feel jealous when they think you are better than them, threatened, entitled, superior, powerful, and intelligent. They act egocentric because of their own lack of creativity, leadership, talent, self-worth, empathy, fears, change, and evolution.

The truth is an imposter copycat created by false narratives, lies, and illusions to maliciously steal creative content and ideas from you, purposely bullying, degrading, and defaming you, slandering you block success, money, and opportunities, and to get the accolades instead of you before anyone else found out.

The butterfly is beautiful only because the caterpillar was brave enough to accept the change. To cure hatred, envy, and jealousy is to see it for what it is: a dissatisfaction with oneself. "Your growth unintentionally invites snakes." You reap what you sow. Let Karma be the righteous

Welcome to the main event. Others are applying pressure, but I will always win!!! The truth is that you chose the wrong team and game and gambled everything. The reality is that you invested in the players of the wrong team and tried to win at all costs, including your soul and success, regardless of the outcome. My soul is not for sale.

You have to cut out the people who hurt you, otherwise you'll get the same version, just in a different face. You also have to cut out the old version who allowed this to happen.

Truth—no one knows the wars she has lived through or the countless battles fought to be here. She manages to share the light and goodness because she knows how it feels to be broken and utterly worthless and doesn't want anyone else to feel the same way. No matter how dark it gets, she smiles

THE ONLY PEOPLE WHO ARE MAD AT YOU FOR SPEAKING THE TRUTH ARE THOSE PEOPLE WHO ARE LIVING A LIE. KEEP SPEAKING THE TRUTH.

Some people create their own storms and then get mad when it rains. Be grateful that the storms should have broken you down, but they opened your eyes. Take that win.

Remember, you're hard to control when you're healthy, happy, and confident. You are hard to manipulate when you have clarity. You're very hard to influence when you have discernment.

When people repeatedly and intentionally undermine your character, integrity, and self-worth, just walk away. How many more chances, how many more times do you allow them to disrespect you? You learned your lessons; walk away.

Once you let go and decide you want a good life, the universe will start moving things to make it happen. The people you need will appear, the healing you need will happen, and the doors you need will open. Once you truly, sincerely decide you are worthy, miracles will flood in.

To everyone who watches my life and gossips about it: don't give up. Season 2 is about to come out. Remember, Karma is the righteous judgment. All the people who celebrated and partied at my downfall, every guilty person who participated will reap what they sow!

Forgive: you are strong when you know your weaknesses. You are beautiful when you appreciate your self-worth and flaws. You are wise when you learn from your mistakes. Your true identity is who you must be, whether you like it or not. Let go of who you thought you were.

The older you get, the more you will learn the value of staying lowkey, of cultivating your circle and only letting certain people in. You can be open, honest, and real while still understanding that not everyone deserves a seat at your table.

When people abandon the people they love, break promises, plagiarize, and tell lies, they abandon the people they're using. That was all the closure I needed. Stay in God's consciousness, take off the unholy masks and rose-colored glasses, and stand in your truth. If your heart is filled with hate and you're blaming anyone, than you are not healed.

The loudest boos will always come from the cheapest seats. The people who invest the least in you will always have the most to say. Trust your work and keep your circle tight. Without trust, you will walk; just remember that you are whole all by yourself.

We are not messing up. You put a lot of energy and effort towards things that failed you, broke you, disappointed you.

We are starting all over: a new page new history, new chapter, new story. Be on the list; be in the top this year!

"Karma Said"

A time will come in your life when some people regret why they treated you wrong. Trust me, it'll definitely come. Be the change. Share to anyone.

Always be ready to survive alone. Some people suddenly change; today you're important to them, tomorrow you're nothing to them. That's real life. Without trust, you will walk—just remember that you are whole all by yourself.

You attract damaged people because your energy is authentically rare, but very healing. A lot of times they end up coming back after they strayed away because they want more access to your energy. That's why you must value your time and energy immensely. Stop being the jumper cables to people who have the energy of a dead car battery...they will literally drain you.

DO NOT ALLOW ANYONE TO BRING YOU BACK TO A LEVEL THAT YOU HAVE ALREADY SURPASSED.

You can be lied to, talked about, and plotted against, and still WIN. When it's your time, it's your time. Your destiny is your destiny. Remember, out of the darkness always comes the light! This is an incredible reminder of the power and strength you hold to survive whatever comes next. You will never forget the sacrifices, lessons, and ability to never give up! Turn your tragedy into triumph.

Not treating them the way they treated you is the way you will receive your blessings! Your Karma is the way you treat them. Their Karma is the way they treated you.

Unfortunately, we no longer have the desire to rebuild bonds we didn't break. You crossed the line. I didn't. And now, I'm good. As I was fighting for you, I realized I was fighting to be lied to; fighting to be taken for granted; fighting to be disappointed; fighting to be hurt again. So, I stopped fighting for you and started fighting to let go.

Next time you're stressed, take a step back, inhale, and laugh. Remember who you are and why you are here. You're never given anything in this world that you can't handle. Be strong, be flexible, love yourself, and love others. Always remember, just keep moving forward! You are not the victim.

There will be people who would rather lose you than be honest about what they have done to you. Everyone has a purpose; you just need to take action to find yours. There will be people who would rather lose you than be honest about what they have done to you. Let go, and let God handle it!

Pray for the peace, patience, healing, protection, and strength to reject, renounce, break, and dissolve every word incantation, negativity, chaos, confusion, trap, hurt, painful lie, hatred, bully, abuse, harassment, slander, obstacle, deception, violence, betrayal, diversion, and spiritual attack, and send it back to the owners. How they treated you is their Karma, and how you treated them is yours.

One of the most attractive things in the universe to a mature person is another person who can accept accountability when calling out their unholy toxic behaviors without deflecting, playing victim, or trying to turn the tables. It's not a loss, it's gaslighting. It's emotional manipulation and abuse.

Be so mentally strong that you can start cutting toxic people off without warning. One of the most attractive things in the universe is a person who can accept accountability without deflecting, playing victim, or trying to turn the tables around. May anything that is bothering you be cleared, healed, solved, and released.

Scientific evidence suggests that there was a miracle. Do you believe in miracles and have strong faith? You can't take the truth, facts, and evidence when we leave this journey. Our hearts are weighed for judgement.

I hope and pray that you see miracles in your life. My family and I are blessed to have seen miracles. We live in peace, love, and faith. We absolutely believe nothing is impossible. I pray that each of you receive a miracle and your purpose.

Facts—narcissists want control over you because all they want is to create illusions, competition, power, and manipulation to win at all costs. They hide behind their masks, ego, toxicity, and arrogance because of their fear of failure, ignorance, cruelty, false promises, accusations, illusions, lack of integrity and empathy, toxic traits, and unholy behaviors. They hide behind their own beliefs because they want to be destroyers and to ruin your life. Narcissists will never admit their crimes or mistakes and only care how sabotage, destroy, blame, and block your success. May anything that is bothering you be cleared and healed.

Keep your distance from people who lie, slander, gossip, bully, cheat, win at all costs, assassinate your character to hide hateful toxic behaviors, threaten, harass, abuse, plagiarize, play the victim, and never admit they are wrong. They always try to make you feel like it's all your fault. Regardless, the truth, facts, and evidence will prevail. Let Karma be the righteous judgement.

Never regret being a good person to the wrong people. Your behavior says everything about you, and their behavior says enough about them. Let Karma be your wrecking ball and divine righteous judgment. Deep down, they really know the truth.

The worst experience is when you keep finding out more about them and you eventually realize that they were never really the people you thought they were. Realty is when you realize the truth about certain people who would never fight battles to protect you and would unjustly sabotage everything to throw you underneath a bus and save themselves.

Remember, it was just a life-changing lesson. Cut the cords to frenemies, enemies, and toxic people, and let Karma be the wrecking ball to righteous judgment. Standing up for yourself doesn't make you argumentative. Sharing your feelings doesn't make you oversensitive. And saying no doesn't make you uncaring or selfish. If someone won't respect your feelings, needs, and boundaries, the problem isn't you; it's them.

Keep your distance from people who lie, slander, gossip, bully, cheat, win at all costs, character assassination to hide hateful toxic behaviors, threaten, harassment, abuse of power, plagiarism, plays victim and will never admit they are wrong who always try to make you feel like it's all your fault. Regardless, the truth, facts and evidence will prevail. May anything that is bothering you be cleared, healed, solved and released.

We have a choice to stop getting angry at their actions and start setting personal boundaries to protect and distance ourselves. You already learned the lesson and know their defense is going to be as draining as the original action that violated these boundaries.

I would rather walk away from someone than be manipulated by an apology that doesn't come with changed behavior. Close the windows, close the gates, close the doors, seal it tight, change the locks, throw away the keys, and never open it again. Every day I wake up, I am grateful for the opportunity, memories, blessings, and prayers for world peace, healing, love, and light.

Remember, you can't really get away from anything and hide from the truth or from the universe. When a leader walks in the room, the followers feel intimidated, and the snakes feel jealous, envious, and threatened, but the next leaders will feel inspired.

Yes, mean girls, we know exactly what you did, and so did the universe. Remember, you can't get away from anything or hide from the truth.

Karma.
What goes around comes around.
Keep your circle positive.
Speak good words.
Think good thoughts.
Do good deeds.

We all have free will to make the right choices and decisions. Your words and thoughts have power. Make sure to speak, think, and act with love, positivity, compassion, and kindness in order to attract blessings into your life. You can't trick the universe.

Today, I pray for you a heart free of sadness, a mind free of worries, a life full of gladness, a body free of illness, and a day full of

God's blessings. LYING ABOUT ME DOESN'T CHANGE THE TRUTH ABOUT YOU. Your truest friends are the people who don't walk out the door when life gets hard. They actually pour some coffee and pull up a chair.

Remember, you can't really get away from anything and hide from the truth or from the universe. When a leader walks in the room, the followers feel intimidated, the snakes feel jealous, envious, and threatened, but the next leaders will feel inspired.

One day you will look back and realize that you worried too much about things that didn't even matter. Everyone is still healing from pain, sorrow, grief, disappointment, loss, sadness, regret, struggle, heartbreak, hurtful moments, and things people said and no longer want to talk about. Time is that most precious gift anyone has. Only light can lead you out of the darkness, and hate cannot drive out hate; only love can do it.

Even when I heard everything you've said about me, I was kind. The lesson is, you can't hide from the truth, trick the universe, or fake it until you make it; you can't cover up or conceal the lies of participation. Regardless of your faith or beliefs, when you glorify deeds for humanity for self-interest, greed, social clout, religion, status climbing, and the desire for respect, these actions must be taken from altruism.

You must demonstrate your work ethic. You cannot possibly think that by mocking God you're going to get anywhere in this lifetime?

Mocking-
Making fun of someone or something in a cruel way; derisive: the mocking hostility in your voice.
Tease or laugh at in a scornful or contemptuous manner: he mocks to make (something) seem laughably unreal.

Let these bad days create your best days. Just because something is over doesn't mean your life is over; this storm did not destroy you, it made you stronger than ever to remind you of what you deserve. This storm will eventually run out of rain. This struggle has broken you and hurt you, but turn this into the best you. I know it seems hard and like it will last forever, but it will eventually run out of rain. This chapter is not your final story. You need to lose what you're settling for to remind you of your own worth.

Remember, they can't possibly believe and think that they can treat others terribly and still receive. The healing journey starts by knowing your self-worth and believing in yourself. We all have free will to make the right choices and decisions. Your words and thoughts have power. Make sure to speak, think, and act with love and positivity, compassion, and kindness to attract blessings into your life. You can't trick the universe.

Today, I pray for you a heart free of sadness, a mind free of worries, a life full of gladness, a body free of illness, and a day full of God's blessings. LYING ABOUT ME DOESN'T CHANGE THE TRUTH ABOUT YOU. Your truest friends are the people who don't walk out the door when life gets hard. They actually pour some coffee and pull up a chair.

Remember, you can't really get away from anything and hide from the truth or from the universe. When a leader walks in the room, the followers feel intimidated, and the snakes feel jealous, envious, and threatened, but the next leaders will feel inspired.

One day, you will look back and realize that you worried too much about things that didn't even matter. Everyone is still healing from pain, sorrow, grief, disappointment, loss, sadness, regret, struggle, heartbreak, hurtful moments, and things people said and no longer want to talk about. Time is that most precious gift anyone has. Only light can lead you out of the darkness, and hate cannot drive out hate. Only love can do that.

Keep your distance from people who lie, slander, gossip, bully, cheat, win at all costs, assassinate your character to hide hateful toxic behaviors, threaten, harass, abuse power, plagiarize, play the victim, and never admit they are wrong, who always try to make you feel like it's all your fault. Regardless, the truth, facts, and evidence will prevail. Let Karma be the righteous judgement.

Giving up is not an option in my book. I will rise, fall, and rise up again even stronger than before. Remember, cheaters think they won the battle, but the realty is that it's all an illusion, because you were always ten steps ahead and knew the truth before they even began the game. A strong person is not the one who doesn't cry. A strong person is one who is quiet and sheds tear for a moment, and then picks up the sword and fights again.

Flowers grow in sunlight, love, light, and where they are watered. Sometimes the grass isn't always greener in someone else's garden. Flowers will never grow in fake artificial sunshine. It depends on the environment and type of soil, and the roots will grow. Flowers will never grow in darkness. A strong person is one who is quiet and sheds tear for a moment, and then picks up the sword and fights again.

It's not too late to eliminate everything that represents falsehoods, because you cannot fake the universe. These are people who pray in church on Sunday but live under a veil of social secrecy, wear a mask, fake being a nice person, lack empathy, hide behind addictions, tell lies, covet lust, and seek revenge, hatred, slander, image defamation, stealing, bullying, bigotry, acts of greed, deception, corruption, bribery for a luxury lifestyle, and the illusion of money.

Let the towers of truth fall and cause the destruction. Know your self-worth to find the courage and strength to move forward. Set your boundaries and move on down the yellow brick road.

Never forget who helped you in difficult times, who left you in difficult times, and who put you in difficult times. Hope is not pretending that troubles don't exist. It is the hope that they won't last forever. That hurts will be healed and difficulties overcome. That we will be led out of the darkness into the sunshine.

Pray, then let it go. Work on yourself and your inner peace. Don't try and manipulate or force the outcome. Trust God to open the right doors at the right time. Giving up is not an option in my book. I will rise, fall, and rise up again, even stronger than before. Remember, cheaters think they win the battles, but in realty, it's an illusion, because you were always ten steps ahead and knew the truth before they even began the game.

A strong person is not the one who doesn't cry. A strong person is one who is quiet and sheds tear for a moment, and then picks up the sword and fights again.

Every day is a new opportunity to never give up and just try harder. You must do the work. Simply renounce any negative influence and the power it may have over me and my life. As above, so below.

Daily affirmations—
I am strong and healed.
I am strong and healed.
I am strong and healed.

Believe and pray to strengthen my spirit and guide me on the path of righteousness, protection, and peace. To grant me the wisdom to discern from the darkness and the strength to resist their influence.

We all have choices. I would rather show people unconditional true love. When someone walks away for peace, it's over. You are seeking people who are worth your time. Love yourself first; everything else will fall into alignment.

Believe in the divine. You can make a change today to make a positive impact towards your beautiful life. Let go of the past. Those people chose to waste their valuable energy and time on chasing toxic addictions, glamorous lifestyles, money, status, and illusions under a false narrative and image. You were never worthy of the life they wanted to live without you, and they sought clout, status, and greed. Under the illusion, there is no one in the universe better than a High Priestess, Empress, Goddess, Royalty, or God's chosen gift.

You Were God's Choice

You can never save them or heal them, and they cannot run from their own Karma. Do not be attached to them. Do not be afraid to heal yourself, and do not become a victim. Be your own dharma.

Time is precious, and so is peace. Let go of what does not serve you anymore. Trust and believe to manifest your destiny.

The worst experience is when you keep finding out more about them and you eventually realize that they were never really the person you thought they were. The realty is, you realized the truth. They were the illusion and were never real soul or person who would fight battles to protect you. They would throw you under a bus to save themselves. This is just a life-changing Karmic lesson.

Cut the cords to frenemies, enemies, and toxic people, and let Karma be the wrecking ball to righteous judgment. There is no reset button on this life or level.

Let love, light, hope, and grace fill every corner of your being, banishing all darkness and fear. Let go of the past you were rescued from because it no longer serves your soul's highest purpose. Your new life is waiting for you, so get excited.

Stay away from low vibrational people who constantly attract a mess, play games, play victims, have not healed from childhood trauma, are sociopathic, negative, or narcissistic, live in the emergency lane, or embody addictions, immaturity, jealousy, envy, deception, drama, and chaos in their lives. Honestly, protect your peace; we do not have any more time to waste on this kind of nonsense. Let go!

She looks nothing like what she's been through, but that woman has fought one million wars and battles, cried to the depths of her soul, and abandoned to broken, and she is still here today, smiling. Your happiness belongs to you and no one else. Never give up, and show up every day. Stay humble and be grateful for the blessings you're going to receive. Love without doubt.

Betrayal and trauma are forms of PTSD. The betrayal of relationships is the most difficult to heal from. How many scars did it take for you to justify because you loved the person holding the knife?

Reality check: if you truly believed they were better than you, then why did you have to hide their relationship, lies, cheating, slander, adductions, defamation, bullying, abandonment, abuse, stolen time, theft, corruption, perjury, and stolen identity to get ahead in this life? You never had the power to give status, title, and rank. It was all an illusion; you were tested and failed miserably.

There are people clapping louder in your corner; just leave the past behind you. Remember, these connections caused too much to repair the damage. They sacrificed you for money, status, clout, and illusions. They had power over a destiny and gifts that never belonged to them. They were yours.

Many people hide behind masks of truth, because of the refusal to accept accountability for the immoral behavior behind closed doors, hideous cruelty, hatred, crimes, lies, and consequences of their actions against innocent people.

Righteous hypocrisy and ignorance lead to the blatant abuse of power in positions that were meant to protect and defend justice and not meant for self-indulgence and greed.

Miracles happen to us every day, but we are so quick to rule out the synchronicity of miracles in our daily lives. We are reminded that we are one world under God, not one nation, not one country, not one chosen people, not one government, not one religion, not one political party, not one belief system. We are one world under judgement.

Civilizations who forgot to take heed and no longer exist include Atlantis, the Romans, and the Egyptian Empire. Religion in biblical times is a reminder how powerful and remarkable God's higher power really is, and if we refuse to change and learn from the past, we will experience the same fate. We can avoid the catastrophe by using the universe's divine gifts to help save humanity and the world. Gifts are not given for selfishness or greed.

We are one world under God. She looks nothing like what she's been through, but that woman has fought one million wars and battles, cried to the depths of her soul, and been abandoned, lied to, and broken, but she is still here today, smiling. Your happiness belongs to you and no one else.

Never give up, and show up every day. Stay humble and grateful for the blessings you're going to receive. Love without doubt.

Stay away from low vibrational people who constantly attract a mess, play games, play victims, have not healed from childhood trauma, and are sociopathic, negative, narcissistic, live in the emergency lane, have addictions, are immature, jealous, envious, deceptive, dramatic, and chaotic. Honestly, protect your peace and don't waste your time on this kind of nonsense. Let go! We do not have any more time.

Let love, light, hope, and grace fill every corner of your being, banishing all darkness and fear. Let go of the past you were rescued from, because it no longer serves your soul's highest purpose. Your new life is waiting for you, so get excited.

Many people hide behind masks of truth because of their refusal to accept accountability for the immoral behavior behind closed doors, hideous cruelty, hatred, crimes, lies, and consequences of their actions against innocent people.

They exhibit righteous hypocrisy and ignorance of blatant abuse of power of positions that were meant to protect and defend justice and were not meant for self-indulgence and greed.

Believe in the devine you can make a change today to make a positive impact towards your beautiful life. Let go of the past. They chose to waste their valuable energy and time on chasing toxic addictions, glamorous lifestyles, money, status, and illusions, all under a false narrative. You were never worthy of the lifestyle they wanted to live without you chasing clout, status, and greed.

You Were the Gift

You can never save them or heal them, and they cannot run from their own Karma. Do not be attached to them when their Karma comes, or you will carry their burdens. Do not be afraid to heal yourself. Time is precious, so protect your peace. Let go of what does not serve you.

Let these bad days create your best days. Just because something is over doesn't mean your life is over. This storm did not destroy you, it made you stronger than ever to remind you of what you deserve. This storm will eventually run out of rain. This struggle broke you and seems like it will last forever, but it will eventually run out of paint. This chapter is not your final story. You need to lose what you're settling for to remind of your own worth.

I fought through the storms that I thought would never end. Don't allow anyone to make you feel guilty for the pain and hurt they caused you. You made it through the storms that made you unstoppable and stronger every day. Stand up and pat yourself on the back for making it through years of abuse by the people you loved the most who were really your enemies.

This was not part of your life's journey; it was meant to cause destruction and disruption from your purpose. God knows the battles, unjust obstacles, challenges, lies, slander, defamation, bullying, harassment, corruption, envy, and jealousy placed by others to disrupt your purpose, divine destiny, and path. You earned every gem in that crown. You are the survivor.

Success is a choice, not a result. Nothing will make you happy until you choose to be happy. Remember, not everyone wants to see you succeed or be happy; it's your choice and decision. When you have a different kind of understanding, you don't even consider them anymore and focus on yourself instead of what others think of you. It's the game changer.

You just take a deep breath and accept it. Move on like you never knew them, because in reality, you didn't.

Know your worth and believe in yourself. It's not your job to validate someone else's worth or constantly validate someone else's perception of you. Symptoms of narcissistic personality disorder in someone else are when you do not feel safe and are being punished by people who lack accountability for their actions, immaturity, emotional manipulation, silent treatment, projections, egotism, happiness hater, ghosting, anger, rejection, deflection of truth, gaslighting, deceit, cheating, contempt, constant sociopathic stalking, online harassment, paid bullying and lies to block you from opportunities, and plagiarism. Apologies without change are just manipulation and lies to cover up corruption, falsehood, theft, and perjury. These are symptoms of narcissistic abuse and behavior.

I chose not to be a victim. I am a kind person. I am all-or-nothing and considerate. I show up and am a genuine, caring, authentic, honest, and reliable person, and I love with all my heart. I am an all-or-nothing kind of person, and they mishandled my love you get to experience the nothingness. There is no in between.

You thought my love was a weakness. Be kind to people, but never allow someone else to mistreat you, hurt you, and hate you. Every day I wake upm I am grateful for the opportunity, memories, blessings, and prayers for world peace, healing, love, and light.

You are incredible! I want you to know that you faced obstacle after obstacle, and you kept handling shit and with a smile on your face, even the days you did not want to get up. God knows you did not deserve any of this and you made it through anyway. Trust and have faith; you made it from the darkness to the light.

You were treated poorly and unfairly, and one day you will look back at the hardest season of your life and be proud and grateful for where you are today. No one deserves to go through what you went through, but you know the truth. You believe that God's here to reckon their sins. Even if they don't believe in God or Karma, the people who kicked you while you were down, who attacked you for no reason, will pay the price.

Keep breathing; they are angry because you know the truth. They could never knock you down and never ever had any power over you; you're still here, and you're not quitting. This narcissistic cult coven will be exposed after they tried to force you to give up in your life. They can send the worst shit to you, and you're still here. You have an amazing life ahead of you.

During times of uncertainty, it can be easy to get lost in our thoughts and worries. We may find ourselves constantly wondering and imagining what the future holds and obsessing over things we cannot control. However, sometimes the best thing we can do is to take a step back, breathe deeply, and trust that everything will work out for the best. By focusing on the present moment and having faith in ourselves and the universe, we can find peace and clarity amidst the chaos.

Remember that life is full of ups and downs, and that every challenge we face is an opportunity for growth and learning. So take a deep breath, let go of your worries, and trust in the journey ahead.

For years, a group thought they had the power to sink my boat, but I chose to keep on rowing. If you are experiencing difficulty, hardships, catastrophic storms, loss, and devastation in your life, it's because of your own negative thoughts, actions, religious beliefs, hatred, slander, harassment, defamation, bullying, envy, jealousy, blasphemy, plagiarism, racism, treason, and low-vibrational energetic thoughts and feelings.

Your life is a reflection mirror and energy magnet of what you send out. It all gets returned to sender. It's ridiculous and slanderous to think a divine being like God used any kind of witchcraft. Your catastrophic hardships are a result of your own bad judgments, poor choices, and decisions.

Where did you plant your seeds? You reap what you sow. Believe that God knows a faking copycat, delusional leader, sociopath, low-vibrational narcissist, Jezebel who spins lies, gossip, or person who commits fraud. You cannot cry over spilt milk after you followed a false narrative.

I am sending love to everyone who is trying to rediscover their voice after life made then believe that silence was safer.

When the original thought or concept, creative style, catch phase, signature, or style, unique to that author is copied using someone else's ideas and creative expression, this is called plagiarism.

Plagarism-
The practice of taking someone else's work or ideas and passing them off as one's own: there were accusations of plagiarism.

I'm sending love to everyone who is trying to rediscover their voice after life made then believe that silence was safer.

Egypt was a highly evolved civilization no longer in existence. History can repeat itself if we do not heed the warnings, evolve, grow, and learn from the mistakes. One humanity, one world, one God.

Remember, Delilah was a liar who secretly spun the truth. She was a femme fatale, an influential saboteur and destroyer who was hired by Sampson's haters, a group of religious enemies, to betray Sampson. He was tested and trusted his secrets to the person he loved with the knowledge of his power. The secret was it was his hair

God gave him to shield him from evil. The snake shared this secret, and it led him towards the destruction of his own fate.

You must not be led by evil false leadership, and you must follow your own principles and values. We all had choices in our life to choose the right path. Do the right thing when you know it's right, because God is watching you.

Pull the weeds and never look back. Let go of the past. Accept the liars as a lesson learned from the illusion. The truth is that you do not know them. Do not feel fear or guilt about leaving everything behind, and move towards your new life.

Do not compromise. Close the door, window, and gate. It's your destiny. You are healed from the pain and illusion and accept what it is never ever going back. You deserve the best. You made the right decisions and choices; do not throw away your future life. Let Karma be the righteous judgement and wrath.

Protect your peace from pettiness and drama-addicted people. You cannot elevate when you spend your lifetime lying, creating friction, chaos, corruption, cheating, slander, theft, criticism, defamation, bullying, gossip, harassment, and stalking. The majority of people drank the toxic Kool-Aid and were lead down the wrong path by a narcissistic, delusional copycat. Say goodbye to people who lost you because of soured lemons when you were the lemonade. One rotten fruit can ruin the entire batch.

Let Karma be their righteous judgement. The Universe is a mirror and reflection of your own creation. We are not the product of our environment, and we have freedom to choose to break Karma's generational curses. We are born into toxic families challenged, and tested with suffering from the poor choices of our parents, poverty, drug and alcohol addictions, physical and mental abuse, pain, heartbreak, mental illnesses, low self-esteem, hatred, depression, anxiety, childhood wounding, and toxic relationships meant to teach us life lessons.

Get over it. You are not unique. Every single person has gone through the awakening of the darkness of the soul. It was your responsibility to learn from it. Do not carry on the same mistakes in this life.

Energy is a powerful force and magnet, so how you think and treat others in this lifetime literally is the Karma you will experience. Treat others with compassion, respect, kindness, and love. The Golden Rule is to treat others however you want to be treated.

I let my guard down and trusted you with my heart when you pulled the rug out. It was you who left me alone, laughed at the pain and betrayal, caused me to be fired at my job, blocked my path, blocked online communication, made false accusations, caused suffering, theft, perjury, greed, corruption, cheating, chaos, control, lust, and affairs, and threw me under bus to hide secrets, character assassination, accusations, accidents, harassment, threats, bloodshed, hateful rhetoric, isolation, breadcrumbs, slander, illegal stalking, abuse, abandonment, and lies for money.

You never cared enough to know if I survived the fallout caused by you. Instead, you chose to play manipulation games, never admitting your wrongdoing and mistakes or apologizing or caring about the bleeding you caused.

It's okay, God knows the truth and heard my cries of desperation and prayers for protection and healing my heart and soul. He dried my tears, gave me peace, and knew whatever hurt you caused me. He healed my heart, cuts, stabs in the back, heartaches, wounds, brokenness, bruises, pain, and tears.

You spent your time covering up your deceit and deception. It's not me you should fear, it's Him. You need to ask forgiveness from God for attacking one of his chosen children.

There is proof of highly intelligent civilizations that no longer exist because their ancestors chose the path of greed, war, repression, hatred, famine, starvation, illnesses, drought, false religion, money, status, power, illusions, and idolization. History repeats itself when we fail to learn from past lessons. Change starts in your own community One humanity, one world, one God.

You deserve fairness and justice for working in a heart space of love and light. The Lord himself goes before you and will be with you. He will never leave you nor forsake you. Don't be afraid. Don't be discouraged. Trust in God. There has to be something in alignment and better for you. You call righteous judgment on this matter.

Always stay humble and kind. It's the answer and solution to all of your trials and tribulations. I have been through the worst storms and suffering in my darkest days. Everyone is tested; let the pressure make you into the rarest diamond. Don't expect a free ride from anyone. You must do the work; you cannot fake God or the universe. One humanity, one world, one God.

Karma will always backfire and return to the owner. You reap the energy you deserve and what you sow. If you are for the community, you are not for me. Righteous judgment must be balanced. Trust, believe, and have faith, even when you feel no one is listening. You can do it. Everything is working on your behalf. Sometimes you're put in places alone so you can realize you do not need anyone but the divine. My timing is just different.

Stand in your truth and tell your story. The divine energy cannot be copied, catfished, or cloaked. When you project negativity, it will immediately return to you. Judgement will be given. One humanity, one world, one God.

They told perfect lies to throw you under the bus, but Karma was the bus driver who ran over their lies. Remember, you can't trick the universe. You reap the energy you deserve and sow.

They are lost souls. Pray that they find healing, light, truth, love, peace, and clarity. Hatred, fears, and ignorance are no excuse. Karmic judgement is their towers, and it's their turn to burn. They had time to learn from their mistakes. The Devil is a liar, and there is no loyalty amongst thieves.

The energy you put out is the same energy you deserve. Instead of wasting your timeline, you could've wished for world peace, harmony, and healing. You will reap what you sow. One humanity, one world, one God.

Perfectly said they told lies to throw you under the bus, but Karma was the bus driver who ran over their deceitful lies. Remember-you can't trick the universe. You reap the energy you deserve and sow.

Karma said, "Sometimes you have to suffer in life not because you were bad, but because you didn't realize where and when to stop being good." Many civilizations thought they were superior and are no longer in existence because they failed to understand universal law, righteous judgement, and Karmic consequences. One humanity, one world, one God.

The Universe and God have removed you from a table where you used to sit in order to save you from harm, hatred, threats, false persecution, accusations, theft, lies, temptation, destruction, and suffering the consequences of other people's poor choices and actions. These people were serving you poison.

History repeats itself when we do not learn these lessons. You deserve the same energy you have given, and you reap what you sow.

Another miracle in plain sight proves that there is a higher civilization. When Daniel was thrown into the lions' den by the king to be devoured because of his faith and belief in God, he emerged from the cage of lions unscathed and protected by the divine.

True altruism is not acting in egotism. One humanity, one world, one God. When there is hatred, envy, fear, competition, greed, contempt, addictions, falsehoods, harm, harassment, violence, resentment, deceit, theft, lying, cheating, corruption and jealousy, this belief does not come from God; it is from your own personal Ego. -ego l'egol noun (plural egos) a person's sense of self-esteem or self-importance: a boost to my ego.

You survived to tell your truth and to share your survival, hidden purpose, and adverse stories. God never believed their false narratives, conspiracy, greed, lies, propaganda, contempt, temptation, addictions, corruption, obsession, slander, bullying, envy, jealousy, harassment, stealing, stalking, bribery, deception, or dark toxic illusions. These are dangerous dark delusions, and they are not from God. He believes in love, peace, kindness, compassion, light, and healing.

The energy you put out is the exact same energy you deserve, and it effects everyone around you. Everything returns to sender and returns to the owner. You cannot run or hide from Karma or the universe.

It's your free will to choose the right path, but it's not rocket science. Who wouldn't want to live in paradise, love, light, healing, happiness, joy, hope and heaven?

You cannot trick the universe, fake it until you make it, be lukewarm, lie about your involvement in wrongdoings, jealousy, envy, intentional deception, hatred, harm others, and pray for salvation without doing the actual work. Karma knows the truth.

It really doesn't matter which religion, Bible, faith, and universal and Karmic laws you practice; just do unto others as you would like to be treated. What you reap is what you sow. Treat others with love and kindness. Be grateful to them for the memories and lessons learned.

Hatred only hurts the soul carrying it. God created men in his own image with love, light, and kindness. It really doesn't matter which religion, Bible, faith, universal and Karmic laws you practice; just treat others as you would like to be treated. What you reap is what you sow. Treat others with love and kindness. Be grateful to them for the memories and lessons learned.

Don't worry, God was never blind to your tears, never deaf to your prayers, and never silent to your pains. He sees the impersonators and frauds who spread hateful rumors, gossip without mercy, lack integrity, lie to cover their participation in duplicitous deeds, deceit, corruption, secrets, betrayals, and abuses of power. Many people act godlike in front of others, but the truth is, they spent their energy on spreading false narratives and lies to lead people down the wrong paths. They are nothing more than scammers and thieves.

People question all the good things they hear about you and believe all the bad in a second. Cowards talk and attack behind closed doors but can never go through the same consequences they put you through. Cowards will destroy your life and refuse to accept accountability for bullying groups. They will dish it out, but they can never go through the same painful experience you endured. They do not have the bravery and courage to change the world. It's easier to destroy, hate, bully, blame others, and ruin somebody else's reputation and life.

Forgiveness is for you to heal your heart, soul, mind, and spirit and to bring you peace. It does not mean that you forgot how you were unfairly treated through lies, betrayals, and heartbreak when all you gave was kindness and love. Some wounds are too deep to heal, so pray to God to lift the burden.

You must face your own demon that you created for yourself. The nature of deception is that we do not realize we are being deceived. Our perception of the truth is misguided and seen through someone else's rose-colored glasses. They tried to falsely portray me when I was a true survivor. Sometimes we must go through darkness in order to appreciate the beauty of light. It was you who voluntarily followed false leadership and the darkness to attack people directly aligned with God. It's up to you how you choose to live and manage your soul today.

"The Nature of Deception"

Through deception, we cannot realize we are being deceived. Our perception of the truth is misguided and seen through someone else's rose-colored glasses. Your actions ty to falsely portray me when I am a true survivor. Sometimes we must go through darkness in order to appreciate the beauty of light. It is up to you how you choose to live and manage your soul today. Do the right thing, even when you believe no one is looking. God knows the truth.

Redemption and salvation occur when you face your own demons. Be careful when you judge others without even knowing them, because you are not defining them. You only define yourself. There are no devils at this ascension level. You must face your own dark choices and decisions. You were intentionally blinded and believed false narratives of hatred, ignorance, deception, deceit, confusion, jealousy, prejudice, chaos, persecution, racism, temptation, lies, fears, and envy. This is the false perception from people who have narcissistic and psychotic delusions about the truth.

Remember, you receive the same energy and Karma you deserve when righteous judgment is called. You cannot hide from your own actions. God is love, compassion, kindness, and forgiveness.

Do you ever feel like you gambled your blessings, rolled the dice, flipped the coin, and chose the illusions of immoral alliances? Did you bet the gold medal on the wrong winning championship team?

We are here to heal, not harm, and love, not hate. We are here to create, not destroy. Don't change so that people will like you. Be yourself, and the right people will love the real you. Be with people who see your soul. Remember, absolutely nothing can grow without sunlight.

We do not have limitations to our blessings. To whom much is given, much is requested. How many times have we self-sacrificed, sabotaged our dreams, or narrowly escaped destruction? After you have faced a life-or-death situation, you have gratitude for every single day in your life. Be fearless; you shall overcome what you are most afraid of to face and confront it in this lifetime.

Trust takes years to build and only moments to destroy. Manipulation is when they blame you for their own mistakes, actions, problems, demons, shadows, toxic and addictive behaviors, poor life choices, wearing a mask, projections, abuse, betrayal, secrets, lies, gossip, slandering, bullying, and false narratives. A narcissist believes their own deception and deceit as truth.

It's like pulling out expired spoiled milk from the refrigerator, smelling it, tasting it, realizing it is spoiled, and putting the carton back, then pulling the same milk carton out again and expecting a different result. It's expired spoiled milk.

God moves you out of the way because he knows you won't move unless your circumstances force you. What you loved the most is taken away from you to appreciate the gift. Once the bridge of trust is broken, it can never be repaired. Remember, trees are pruned to remove the dead and decaying leaves and branches so that beautiful growth can begin. Let the decaying leaves fall away, and trust the process.

When you're on the divine path, you are given the gifts of discernment to guide you on this journey. I love whenever I get the heads-up from the universe way before the enemy's attacks and know the enemy's next move before it happens.

You see, the entire time, you were under an illusion and thought the game played was checkers, when at a higher level, we were playing chess.

We are never stuck in spiritual contracts or commitments. When it was you who helped violate and destroy Gods destiny, purpose, and plan, all terms, principles, and conditions must be fulfilled. A new contract will begin, and fate will be fulfilled.

Disclaimer: Conditions of agreements are common sense. Does it make sense to receive blessings, gifts, status, clout, money, power, and rewards when you failed to follow the terms and conditions of the contract? You cannot revoke, revise, mimic, replace signed parties, replace with non-divine partners ordained by spiritual law, mock God, and believe He does not see the truth. Do you believe you will receive divine blessings?

Do you believe you will receive blessings when it was you who agreed to participate in theft, chaos, hostility, gossip, bulling, hatred, false accusations, harassment, secrets, blame, addictions, and greed?

Do you really believe you will receive divine forgiveness, salvation, and blessings when it was you who teamed up as a community, signed NDA's, accepted bribes to cause chaos, blocked employment opportunities, allowed online stalking, harassment, unlawful hacking, slander, perjury, copycat retaliation, revenge, retribution, mail tampering, stealing identity, fraud, theft, wrongful accusations, lies, adultery, envy, jealousy, contempt, bullying, false misinformation, hate, deceit, saddictions, abuse of authority, and defamation of character to cause harm and punishment on an innocent person?

Remember, God is the creator of all things and rules over the illusions of darkness. There is no higher power than God, period. You receive the same energy and lessons you deserve. You do not get a hall pass on Karma.

Finding yourself consists of peeling off of social and childhood conditioning. Forgive your parents; they were learning, too! It's time to heal our inner child's wounding. Every woman that heals herself helps heal generations of women who came before her and all the women who will come after her. Pray for world peace and inner childhood.

Mirror, mirror, on the wall, I'll always get up after I fall. We are supposed to be mirrors of grace, love, light, compassion, and kindness to others. Mirrors never lie, yet we believe the false illusions, narratives, and perceptions based on the immoral egregious behavior we want to see. This image is manipulation and not reality. You cannot heal people who love to be sick. Mirrors never lie, and the truth burns up the lies. Karma is the same energy you deserve. Be fearless and know that your truth will expose the lies. You survived to tell your story; never underestimate your own truth.

Be fearless in knowing that the truth will expose the lies. You survived to tell your story; remember, documentation is better than convincing conversations. Close the window, close the gate, close the portals, close the door. Seal it tight, never to opened again. You have no power here. I am strong and healed. I rebuke any and all darkness and negative energy and transcend it, return it back to the owner. Return it back to sender. Righteous judgment is called.

On your healing journey, use the following prayer: "God, close the windows, close the gates, close the portals, close the doors, and seal them tight, never to open again. You never had power or control over me. I am strong and healed. I rebuke the darkness and negative energy, and I transcend it, return it back to the owner. Return it back to sender, and let righteous judgment be called." Amen

When someone else tries to control your path and mess up your life, stay calm and meditate. Don't engage in their same behavior. Let the negativity go, and don't let the hateful energy distract you. Every day, call righteous judgment. Step aside and let Karma handle it.

Be fearless; it's the only thing keeping you from growing, learning the lessons needed to succeed, and moving forward. Hearing the truth is hard and tastes a lot like vinegar, but the story must be told. If anyone uses fear, rhetoric, lies, hate, violence, identity theft, threats, bullying, or hidden immorality as a strategy to get their people to work, that person is not a leader.

Think about the time and money they wasted on negative energy hide behind their religion, ideology, politics, deceit, corruptions, and ignorance that could've been spent building lives, healing, and changing the world. The energy you spend is the same energy you receive.

Hurt people hurt people, and healed people do not harm anyone; they heal others. If you feel hate, jealousy, depression, anger, envy, judgment, insecurity, wounded, greed, fear, lust, addictions, discrimination, guilt, lies, or shame, these feelings and actions are not from God. God is loving, fearless, compassionate, forgiving, caring, and kind. You attract the same energy that you deserve.

No one has the power over the narrative of your truth and story. They lack maturity and accountability and will create and make up a narrative about you so they don't feel bad about what they did to you when you did not deserve it. You have power to control your own narrative. Always tell your truth; it's your narrative and story, and you'll be free.

Be aware that words and thoughts are very powerful. Believe in yourself. I was never an option; I was always the leader, not a follower. I was always the first choice. Take your power back to make changes, speak the truth, and to control your own life choices, because one else can do it for you. If you are a person who betrays a code of honor, then you are nothing more than a coward who can't lead their own life or make their own choices, and you live through someone else's perception.

We are the wisdom keepers who bring knowledge and the truth tellers of the world. Yes, we already know. Be kind to everyone. What you planted spiritually is the harvest you're going to receive. The energy you put out is the same energy you deserve. If you choose not to plant the seeds of abundance, prosperity, kindness, and love or to water the spiritual garden, then your lineage will be cursed with hardships and financial bankruptcy. Remember, absolutely nothing can grow in darkness.

If you chose to be a thief who stole, lied, and cheated for an illusion of inheritance through your life, then your future is cursed. How did you treat others while you were here is the Karma you deserve.

Yes a Masters 33. I pray you heal from the things no one ever apologized for. We can't control what other people do, say, or believe, but we can control how we react. How we react is our Karma; how they react is theirs. The cheat code is to know what they did to you and give them grace, kindness, love, and peace, because you don't want the bad Karma to backfire and return to sender onto and your family.

There will be punishment tor their terrible deeds and crimes against an innocent person. Have faith that God will stop the unfair attacks of warfare and hatred, biases, harassment, bullying, slander, false reporting, misinformation, gossip, lies, greed, corruption, and defamation against innocent people.

It takes grace to remain kind during cruel situations. Call righteous judgment and allow Karma to take control over them and anyone else involved.

You Cannot Run from Karma

Acting in your ego and abusing power is a detriment to society. Discrimination, retaliation, wrongful termination, bullying, ageism, filing unlawful claims, stalking, cruelty, abuse of power, misconduct, complaints, harassment, jealousy, and grievances against an innocent person to hide your wrongdoings is a criminal legal offense. This was done to hide their legal repercussions, misconduct, and unethical conduct and behavior. They wear a mask of integrity.

I visited dirt church today. It was a beautiful walk. We either live, grow, heal, glow, and evolve, or we go. Use the same storm you're going through to keep growing and water your soul. Remember, dirty water doesn't stop plants from growing, so don't let hatred, jealousy, envy, ego, fears, failure, falsehoods, or negativity stop your progress. It will take 67 days for change to happen.

Interestingly, God's love, grace, kindness, freedom, compassion, miracles, healing, and blessings are free and only cost us a prayer. As far as I know, he doesn't own a bank account, so where are the tithings going to serve humanitarian purposes?

Is the outdated policy now used to justify power, status, political affiliations, influence, control, and wealth for the masses, or is it used by elites to support their agenda and own interests and pockets? I do not believe Jesus or the disciples ever gave a tithing. One world, one humanity, one God.

Master Number 33, High Priestess, Empress, Earth Angel, Starseed, Indio Child, and Shaman Healers are given by the most high God. Your lineage must earn this status, and the Master Teacher is the most spiritually evolved of the Master Numbers. It boosts the powers of the numbers that came before it to new heights and possesses the ability to bestow knowledge and truth on to others.

So now you know who is on my spiritual team and who is telling the truth. Believe that everything is seen and recorded for righteous judgment and Karma.

I do not regret my past or the precious time I wasted with the people who did not value me. This was a lesson I needed to learn. Life humbles you when you realize how much time was wasted on people you can't build a foundation with. So, she stopped waiting for a hero, picked up her own sword, and slayed the dragons and demons herself.

Remember, if you can't build with them, they can't go with you to the next level. It's time to leave their burdens behind. You are not responsible for their actions. Time thieves are only holding you back from your own success.

The universe believes that time thieves should be held accountable for their actions and broken spiritual contracts. There are no do-overs, rewrites, or redos in life when it was you who chose the wrong path. Forgive, let go, stand aside, and let Karma be the wrecking ball in their lives.

Ever feel like you followed the Pied Piper down the wrong yellow brick road? A community was sold an illusion of broken promises, luxurious lifestyles, and a life lacking morality, filled with indulgence and gluttony, and orchestrated by the Devil. The community hires a mysterious stranger known as the Pied Piper, who possesses a magical pipe. With his enchanting music, the Piper lures the rats and snakes away, leading them to drown in the river.

However, when the community refuses to pay the agreed-upon fee for his services, the Piper takes revenge. On a Sunday, while the inhabitants are in church, he plays a different tune that mesmerizes the town's children. The children follow him out of the community and into a cave, which mysteriously closes behind them. The children are never seen again.

The tale serves as a cautionary story about the consequences of breaking promises, telling lies, and cheating, and importance of keeping one's word. The community is left with regret and is now haunted by the memory of the Pied Piper and the loss their children.

Oppression happens when we don't take the time to heal ourselves and focus on the future rather than focus on our purpose.

Always follow your own North node and compass, not someone else's religion or political beliefs, because neither one really matters. One God, one world, one humanity. A visionary sees what will be and what is. Let it go, and stop showing them that you'll stay through anything.

The altered facts and evidence, coordinated efforts of isolation and intimidation, ostracization, corruption in correspondence,, falsified documents, lies, character assassination, ego, identity fraud, stalking, slander, bullying, jealousy, hatred, harassment, propaganda, perjury, accusations, illegal misconduct leading to mitigation, theft of proprietary ideas and concepts, plagiarism, and blocking opportunities to hide the hidden truth. Let Righteous judgment and Karma be the wrecking ball in their lives.

Keep in mind, the Devil is a narcissistic pathological liar who believes he has control over your narrative and your story. There are only two ways this narrative works or can influence a human behavior: through manipulation tactics or through inspiration. Manipulative spirits deflect when they are caught up in their manipulative lies. They deflect accountability of their deception and actions by creating false narratives, propaganda, lies, Pandora's box, chaos, revenge, bigoted hatred, jealousy, envy, spite, slander, harassment, defamation of character, bullying, and fodder to hide their rock throwing. They act innocent of any wrongdoing to hide their involvement in deceit and participation in attacking an innocent person.

A God complex is consistently inflated feelings of personal ability, privilege, or infallibility. One God, one world, one humanity.

Demonstrate your power and rebuild your life. If I can survive the challenges, obstacles, devastation, rocks, attacks, sticks, stones, storms, floods, and towers sent to destroy me, then I believe you have the courage to stand up and fight back against unjust actions.

My secret weapons are prayer, faith, strength, confidence, and wearing God's armor as a shield. You were saved to share your survival stories.

Be too busy working on your own grass and watering it daily to be concerned if your grass is any greener somewhere else. Focus on your own joy, happiness, and journey. Don't waste valuable energy and time comparing yourself to others. You will never compare.

You wouldn't invite a thief into your house, so why would you allow a thief to steal your happiness, joy, and journey? Besides, thieving is a crime against spiritual, religious, universal, and judicial laws. At the end of this journey, what lessons will the thieves gain from copying someone else's life story and essence? Let righteous judgment prevail, and Karma will be their consequence.

The grass was only greener because it was artificial turf. You chose to build a foundation on fake grass. If you failed to plant the seeds in the soil and water the grass, then don't be upset when nothing grows but weeds.

I went to the Dirt Church on Sunday and had another amazing walk. They can huff and puff to try to blow your house down, but it will depend on your strength, faith, and devotion to God. How was your house built on a foundation of soil, straw, and wood, or of stones, concrete, and positive spiritual growth amidst the underlying chaos, destruction, and decaying darkness?

In light of what is currently happening in society, it is a huge reminder to treat your mind, spirit, soul, and body as a temple, not a visitor center. Attachments are sacred, and soul connections and cannot be discarded.

The solution is celibacy and avoiding unwanted attachments, sickness, suffering, and illnesses. A protected divine can never transfer or transmute diseases. Guilt and shame are wasted emotions. Forgive, let go, and let Karma be their wrecking ball in their lives.

Karmic law states that you reap and receive the exact same energy you put out. Everything returns to sender when divine justice is called.

Spiritual court is in session—remember that all is recorded for the accuracy of Karmic justification. How did you spend your time here? Righteous judgement is called for deflecting your participation in paid bullying, lies, online stalking, mail tampering, perjury, plagiarism, identity theft, obstruction, reckless conduct, evidence of harm, betrayal, attempt to destiny swap for inheritance, lies about how you contracted a sickness, secret society cult, greed, corruption, group sexual activity, abuse of power, chaos, addictions, retaliation, slander, defamation of character, persecution, revenge, harassment, happiness haters, manipulation, and mental health issues.

It sounds like a Dateline movie, but is the truth, believe it or not. It is clear who was the menace to society and who was the innocent victim.

What does Genesis 19:22 teach us? These Bible verses remind us that when God rescues us from harm and instructs us to never go back again because you will turn into a pillar of salt, He meant it. Everyone is tested to ensure we learn from the lessons. If we continue to defy his commands, there are repercussions for defiance. God, if I'm chasing or going the wrong direction, please realign me. I am finally learning how to let go. Please do not let history repeat itself.

It's no fun when the rabbits go to the gun, and you have to run. Do not run. It's your opportunity to learn, grow, evolve, shine, and glow, or you will go. Even a lump of coal when pressured becomes a beautiful diamond, and a piece of sand turns a pearl when you face your problems instead of running away from them.

The same boiled water hardens an egg and softens a potato. Working through these pressures instead of running from situations or conflicts is what makes you stronger. Teaching yourself compassion makes you ready for an extraordinary destiny.

Soap box message of righteous judgment: we follow leaders as idols who have never proven themselves and hold the illusion of power. They preach that they stand for the cause of the world, but God but does not own a home, car, business, or bank account.

These false leaders promise to fight against corruption, care about global climate and world peace, and support freedom and democracy for all citizens, yet what actual work efforts did you perform to earn your status and ranking or help the people?

It seems we are focused on a society of teaching leaders how to deceive, cause segregation, manipulate, hide secrets, blackmail, blame, spread conspiracy, spread social media propaganda, cheat, steal, profit, plagiarize, steal, hate, practice corruption, and spread lies to hide their own lack of accountability regarding knowledge of the deceptions pertaining to injustice and greed. One God, one humanity, one world.

Any position, status, wealth, and fundamental rights should be weighed against how you helped humanity. What work did you accomplish and put in to earn wealth? When you have wealth and power, you are tested. Did you serve humanity or yourself?

Why do we have all of the layers of bureaucracy? What really matters at the end of this journey is that your soul and heart are measured. You do not own a bank account in heaven. Be the change for the world, not for yourself.

Lucifer/Satan/Devil/Demon/Witch/Warlock/Magician/Cults/Secret Society/False Practitioner/Energy Vampires are the greatest liars and shapeshifters of all time. Satan lived in the garden of Eden and was cast out of heaven after his betrayal and defiance of God.

No one has dominion over your soul except God. No one has the power of salvation over your soul except God. Wake up and smell the coffee; you are smarter than these delusional beliefs. Satan's job was to manipulate you into believing he was in control and had power over your soul, but you actually work for God.

Find the glitch in the matrix. Satan's duty is to bring you into sin, greed, gluttony, chaos, addictions, death, self-destruction, misery, madness, despair, shame, temptation, fear, sadness, manipulation, break loving connections, hate, and harm, and to give up on your dreams instead of simply asking God for forgiveness. You are tested every day.

There is absolutely no escape clause, zero regrets, and no second chances. You cannot escape from the truth. Stand in your power and tell the world your story. Let righteous judgment prevail, and Karma be served.

You cannot carry other people's burdens up that hill. They must carry their own responsibilities, decisions, choices, challenges, and judgment. Chosen ones have an undeniable faith and power over fear. We know our destiny and purpose and are the true believers that nothing from your past determines who you are today.

The bridges burned from the past are from the choices made. It is not worth the effort and time to rebuild. I pray that we break every barrier, holding up your prosperity and flooding your life with abundance.

Dirt Church: They built a false house of cards using your mystic abilities…the collapse and destruction have begun. A divine alchemist, you can consume the dark and convert it to light by using love, healing, kindness, compassion, courage, and peace.

The darkness can teach you things about yourself that the light never could. Remember, it is better to create something of your own accord than nothing at all and criticize others.

If you blindly followed, believed, or acted without unjustified evidence in favor of hatred, bigotry, obstruction of justice, stalking, criminal behavior, accusations, falsifying documents, perjury, harassment, theft, corruption, and witnessed intimidation or bullying without knowing the truth, your Karma is the same persecution and oppression.

Has anyone ever asked the direct question, "Why in the world did you believe fake information, false narratives, gossip, conspiracy, and propaganda without evidence on an innocent person?"

You cannot stick your heads in the sand and pretend you knew nothing about the unlawful treatment. Righteous judgment is called by God, and Karma, and spiritual, religious, and universal laws must be followed. You refusing to acknowledge their wrongdoings and believing false narratives does not give you a pardon.

Karma is their righteous judgment. Leaders in secret societies attack the whistleblowers' and truth-tellers' integrity when their corrupt actions are exposed, and they willfully disregard them. Behind closed doors, they plot, plan, participate in bullying, manipulation, intimidation, discrimination, stealing, plagiarism, harassment, stalking, exploitation, biases, and violence, and create false accusations and lies to justify their transgressions of innocent people.

If you know about it, then talk about it. You do not get a free pass. Say no to practices that are deceptive, exploitative, or harmful when everyone else believes the false narrative is true and everything is fine.

All greatness teeters on whether a hero overcomes the terror and fear within and advances regardless of the circumstances. To survive, I prefer to have undeniable faith in God than follow a recipe for failed corrupt leadership.

An apology without change and pure intentions is just another form of manipulation and excuse. It doesn't matter how dirty others may play; Karma has a big bite. Always move with pure intentions. Change happens the minute you decide you want better for yourself, and then the entire universe begins to shift in your favor.

You have the freedom to say no to toxic people and situations in your life whenever it no longer serves your higher purpose. If I was ever an option in your life, then never choose me. Silly rabbit, tricks are for kids. It's an insult and a ridiculously absurd illusion to believe I would ever compete or compare to anyone else in the universe. Let me be honest, you never had the power over me because I was never an option.

I chose faith in God and healing myself from childhood wounds, trauma, and painful chapters in my life. I am never an option. You deserve people in your life who don't have misconstrued ideas about you. Don't talk about it, be about it.

You may not bear false witness against anyone, or you will pay the ultimate consequences and bear the same Karma. Do not sell your soul to anyone, and always tell the truth.

Drama is DEMONIC. Gossip is DEMONIC. Slander is DEMONIC. Pathological liars are DEMONIC. Narcissists are DEMONIC.

Accusation is DEMONIC. Speaking ill behind the back of a brother or sister in Christ is STRAIGHT UP WITCHCRAFT.

Always tell your truth and let Karma be the wrecking ball and destruction in their lives when righteous judgement is called.

An apology without change and pure intentions is just another form of manipulation and excuse. It doesn't matter how dirty others may play; Karma has a big bite. Always move with pure intentions. Change happens the minute you decide you want better for yourself, and then the entire universe begins to shift in your favor.

You have the freedom to say no to toxic people and situations in your life whenever it no longer serves your higher purpose. If I was ever an option in your life, you then never choose me. Silly rabbit, tricks are for kids. It's an insult and a ridiculously absurd illusion to believe I would ever compete or compare to anyone else in the Universe. Let me be clear: I was never an option. I chose faith in God and healing from the trauma and pain in my life. I am never an option. You deserve people in your life who don't have misconstrued ideas about you. Don't talk about it, be about it. When your intentions are pure, you do not need worry. Just focus and have faith.

What legacy did you leave behind? What is your Hallmark card? What seeds of growth did you leave? What if you never jumped off that cliff towards destiny or experienced anything in life because you feared what someone else thought about you, and you feared change?

In 100 years from now, you will not wake up worrying if anyone liked your pictures or opinions. Lifecycles are short; paint those pictures, jump off those cliffs, be fearless to fly, and plant those seeds. No one has the power to make your decisions in life. No more would've, should've, could've. You may never get the chance again.

Stop giving CPR and breathing life back into dead situations, past trauma, childhood wounds, and people you have already learned lessons from. Karma must be balanced, so if you failed the test, you must redo the cycle.

Do not follow the advice of others sitting on the sidelines of life who have never had the power over you. Don't be misled; the truth is that being around bad company corrupts people's character. Adam and Eve knew the garden of Eden's rules about temptation, and when you intuitively know it's not right, then you have a choice to make.

You can choose to say NO and not bite the poisonous apple. Don't listen to a snake, use your discernment, have situational awareness, learn from past mistakes, and continue to grow and evolve. Let go of the people who no longer serves your higher purpose, and decide not to be around the temptation. Our weaknesses are always tested.

Guilt and fear are wasted emotions, and you cannot blame others for your own failures. Never stop being a good person with a loving heart. I know it can be hard and it can hurt sometimes to resist the temptation to become a cold-hearted soul. Remember, it's kind people like you who are needed so much more than lying, cold-hearted snakes, and kind souls are destined to heal and change the world.

Anger and fear are like fire. Uncontrolled, this energy can burn the whole world up. Do not mistake this fallacy as strength. It is a powerful emotion in place of another underlying and unchecked emotion. The feeling of envy, jealously, brokenhearted, sadness, hurt, shame, pain, fear, grief, betrayal, greed, guilt, lack, deceit, embarrassment, ego, contempt, confusion, corruption, uncertainty, depression, despair, ignorance, lust, and loss are all false emotions.

The "give it to me or I'll take it" mindset has destroyed too much in this world. This unchecked energy has weakened the entire world's system, which desperately needs to balance. Focus on how you can control your own positive creations, community growth, peace, kindness, compassion, righteous justice, unconditional love, hugs not drugs, harmony, and healing. One God, one world, one humanity.

What if we lived in a different universe where the people were paid for their humanitarian services they provided instead of their religion, status, clout, morality, money, greed, baptism, charity donations, tithes, judicial rank, race, military power, political influence, and party? There is only one way to the kingdom of heaven, and it's through salvation and love, and definitely not through your own bank account. Remember, our souls and hearts are weighed at the end of the journey. I am rateful to live the life I chose, and I never settled for less.

What legacy will you be remembered for 10 years from now? Redemption is earned when you can see yourself as a blessing and face your own challenges, problems, failures, and demons that blinded you. Unfortunately, many of you ignored the red flags and warnings regarding the choices you made today.

Start to heal and cleanse your mind, body, spirit, heart, soul, and whatever it takes to transform. First, start by cleaning out your own house and take out the lying, trashy, low-level harems of Karmics, Delilahs, and Jezebels, regardless of gender. Their only purpose is to prey upon your weaknesses, destroy spiritual contracts, and deliberately delay your healing to miss out on your abundance opportunities. Karmics, Jezebels, and Delilahs work for the wrong team and are never allowed in the kingdom.

It is ridiculous embarrassing to display arrogance, ego, and blasphemy, regardless of which faith and religion you believe in. it is all a grand master illusion. Your choice is, "It's God's way, or it's the highway."

To start the healing process, avoid toxic substances and cleanse your mind, body, spirit, heart, and soul. Do whatever it takes to protect your health from toxic behaviors and substances, to transcend and transform. Second, clean out your own closets by taking out the garbage: lying, trashy Karmics, Delilahs, and Jezebels, regardless of their gender.

Their only purpose is to lower your energy by preying on your weaknesses, spreading lies and illnesses, and delaying your healing to miss out on life's opportunities. Remember, the Karmics, Jezebels, and Delilahs play for the wrong team and are never allowed in the kingdom.

It's ridiculous, embarrassing, arrogance, ego, blasphemy, regardless of which faith, cult, secret society and religion you believe your above protection laws. It's all a grand master illusion. Your choice is "It's Gods way or it's the highway.

New World Enlightenment means that you take full responsibility for your own destiny, actions, and life. What if we lived in a society without politics, biblical history, isolation, power, religion, shared resources, and paid-for efforts to help humanity? One world, one God, one humanity.

Spirituality does not come from religion. It comes from our soul. We must stop confusing religion and spirituality. Religion is a set of rules, regulations, and rituals created by humans, which were supposed to help people's spiritually. Due to human imperfection, religion has become corrupt, political, divisive, and a power struggle.

Spirituality is not theology or ideology. It is simply a way of life, pure and original as given by the most high God. Spirituality is a network linking us to the most high God.

You survived to tell your truth and story. You chose not to be a victim, and you get up, show up, and give hope to others going through their darkest moments. Evolve, grow, and change, or you will you go. It's God's way or the highway. It's an illusion to believe you had control and power over anyone else, especially a catfish con-artist thief who bragged to others about their malicious behavior and actions towards others. You were given enough fishing line to catch them in their own deceptive net of lies.

Break the chains of injustices and heal the generational curses from your childhood wounds. When tyrants ask you to yield and protect their lying and unjust deeds, it's the first link for the chain that will eventually hold you in bondage.

If you stood by and knew about this atrocity and failed to help and did nothing, then you deserve the same Karma. You do not get merit for not participating in the heinous actions. You were tested to see if you would do the right thing and tell the truth. That's how pain pattens get passed on generation after generation. Break the chain today. Meet anger with sympathy, contempt with compassion, cruelty with kindness. Greet grimaces with smiles. Forgive and forget about finding fault. Love is the weapon of the future.

Dirt Church Sunday: You are free to choose, but you are not free from the consequences of your choices. We must pay the price of your decisions though Karma.

It's a dangerous way of thinking when we allow decisions made by people who lack accountability, respect, integrity, morality, honesty, abuse of authority, power, and greed to feel like they are above judiciary consequences from their own actions. If you chose to treat others like a sacrifice and believe you will gain influence, power, and wealth, then don't be surprised when Karma is balanced, and the same poisoned water and actions are returned to you. What you give is the same exact outcome you deserve.

The Maya, Israelites, Babylonians, Aztecs, Ancient Egyptians, Romans, Canaans, Olmecs, Toltecs, Teotihuacans, and Celts all believed in sacrificial practices and prayed to idols, fallen angels, and false gods, and they met the same fate and demise. History will repeat itself if we continue this path and the same destructive behavior. One world, one God, one humanity.

When you wear the armor of God and his children, covering yourself with his light and love, who could ever be against you? Be in your North node, not your South node, and miracles will happen for you, too.

Let go of the fear and false narratives, egocentric religious beliefs meant to segregate, wars meant to control conquer and divide, outdated ideology of destruction for greed, and useless political rhetoric and propaganda.

You were meant to lead others, not follow the same destructive path and logic of failure. Do not drink the same poisonous Kool-Aid. History has proven itself wrong, so believe that there's only one master in control.

When you wear the armor of God and shield yourself with His love and healing light, who can stand against you? Learn to be strong and be in control of your own destiny. One God, one world, one humanity.

Everyone is watched by the most high God. You have heard it said that a just king gives stability to his nation, but one who demands bribes destroys it! For decades, bribes have blinded the clear-sighted and subverted the cause of those who are in the right.

Those who have accepted the bribes in secret to pervert the ways of justice will receive the same deserved punishment.

Many people in power have companions of thieves. They love bribes and run after gifts. They were tested and failed miserably to bring justice for humanity, and they only serve themselves and will be punished. Anyone who takes a bribe to support coercion, corruption, hatred, or cause harm to innocent people will experience the same consequences Those who have taken bribes will be exposed and brought to justice for all to see.

Those who walk righteously and speak with sincerity will be blessed. Those who reject unjust gain will be granted a gift from above. For those that shake their hands so that they hold no bribes, those who stop the bloodshed. One world, one God, one humanity.

Think of yourself as a human energy source that can heal your own heart, health, mind, body, and soul. We are all one connected consciousness that influences the energy in our entire universe, not just in your community. A ripple effect of negative energies or positive energies can impact the entire universe's balance. Everything is connected and controlled by your triggered emotions.

To raise to a higher consciousness and vibration, be aware of your emotions. The biggest investment you can make right now is in controlling your own thoughts. Be aware of your own frequency, because it can affect healing. You cannot heal without a filter of imbalance.

There's always something to be grateful and thankful for. Your triggers are your responsibility to heal. To help heal yourself, meditate using high-frequency intensity, exercise, and mindfulness. One world, one God, one humanity.

I am grateful every day for my healing journey and protection from all the demons stalking me. They are not as strong as the angels protecting me. Through your darkest times, always remember to have unconditional love and faith. God gives his hardest battles to his strongest warriors.

The Ethiopian Bible scrolls predate all versions of the original bible by 2000 years. Within this version, it gives an entirely different interpretation of religious doctrine believed today. It begs the following questions: why was this Bible banned and hidden from man? Who gave the churches the right to hide the truth from all people on earth? Which religion is the truth?

The Book of Enoch is a terrifying read in some sections. Another set of fallen angels rebelled against God after they were cast out of heaven because of their defiance of God with Satan. Enoch was a profit of God He gave His divine trusted messages to. Enoch is the great grandfather of Noah. God asked him to tell the fallen angels of his plans of destruction due to their defiance.

Just like Adam and Eve, the fallen angels had free will to make their choices but knew the consequences of their actions. As predicted and foretold, the floods came with a fierce vengeance to cleanse the world of their sins. Enoch's revelations brought the apocalyptic destruction to the world by destroying the fallen angels who defied God. This book is shocking.

I am so grateful and thankful for the most high God, Holy Spirit, and divine guides who have ordered my steps every day. It's an undeniable feeling of gratitude, hope, and love I've had since I was a child, knowing I was divinely protected and safe. When I am with friends taking pictures, I always laugh and tell them that if they see things in their pictures, it's just me and my angels. I know that during my darkest times when people tested my heart and faith the most, I prayed for guidance from the Holy Spirit and most high God.

So, I Do Believe in Miracles

Yes, I am a walking testimony of miracles that happened to me and caused me to have trust, faith, love, and courage. This little light of mine, I am going to let shine, let it shine, let it shine. Every day I wake up and get up, I am thankful and grateful He chose to save and heal me from the pits of darkness, pain, suffering, despair, sexual abuse, misery, car accidents, evilness of people, disease, sadness, grief, sickness, injuries, poverty, poisoning, depression, bullying, bullets, death, and countless life-threatening situations I have survived. How many miracles can I save you from before you believe?

When I travel, I always go to the congregation of that city's or country's faith, whether it's a religious temple, cathedral, mosque, chapel, church, or pulpit. I pray to the most high God and Holy Spirit and light a candle. I pray for world peace, love, light, and healing, and I am thankful to God for the protection given to me. Every day is a miracle, and so many times in my lifetime, I could tell you

I received a gift of a miracle, look up and say to God, "I know, God, that was you, and I am forever grateful."

Healing has been in the family, and I have always been my mom's student when she passed her exams. I remember attending many healing sabbaticals and building Indian sweat lodges with lava rocks for purification. Jacob and I visited the world-famous Therapy on the Rocks in Sedona, Arizona, with John Barnes, the creator of Myofascial healing.

I spent an entire day with John Barnes in the Sedona Desert learning about the power of vortex energy and that every living organism is connected. Together, John and I touched a centurion cactus, and it sent a huge explosion of energy and aura captured on film. Later, he sent me a copy to inspire me on my own sabbatical journey.

Beware and use your own discernment regarding the imposters and scam artists. God is going to send you to places you didn't feel qualified to go when you follow your North node and divine purpose. He doesn't call the qualified; he qualifies the called. Everyone is tested on this journey. The imposters wear the masks of integrity and morality, but it's all an illusion.

Cut people off who no longer serve your higher purpose, who wasted their time and energy on spreading false narratives and gossip. This behavior is considered low-vibrational energy and trauma bonding. Protect your peace of mind from someone who does not value your worth. You cannot control someone else's fears, emotions, actions, jealousy, envy, and insecurities. This is projection of their own feelings onto you.

Just simply walk away from situations or people who threaten your peace of mind and self-respect, devalue your feelings, who refuse to grow up, take responsibility for their actions, or change. Never feel guilty for cutting someone off who does not know your self-worth and who cursed themselves for their own selfish actions, betrayal, harm, corruption, lying, and hatred that they treated you with in this lifetime. Everyone must take accountability for their own shortcomings, mistakes, and failures.

Do not waste your pearls on swines, Jezebels, sirens, and sewer maidens. The reality is that they have really low vibrational energy. Step aside and let Karma prevail.

The Book of Enoch is still very clear that if you choose to defy or violate laws, then your punishment for your misconduct will be an eye for an eye. Under righteous judgment, you deserve the exact same punishment. You cannot hide from your own actions because it is the exact same energy you put out.

If you watched, participated, hid corrupted evidence, online group stalking, malicious accusations, sabotage, forged inheritance records stolen property, payments, shadow banning, perjury, illegal surveillance, plagiarism, fraud, identity theft, slander, bullied, signed NDA received, bribery, knew and kept silent then you will receive the same Karma.

> *But with the righteous He will make peace and will protect the elect, and mercy shall be upon them.*
> *And they shall all belong to God, and they shall all be prospered, and they shall all be blessed. And He will help them all, and light shall appear unto them, and He will make peace with them. And behold! He cometh with ten thousands of His holy ones to execute judgement upon all and to destroy all the ungodly: And to convict all flesh of all the works of their ungodliness which they have ungodly committed, and of all the hard things which ungodly sinners have spoken against Him.*

Welcome back to the Big Top Circus. Step right up and don't be shy. It's not my monkey, it's not my circus, but we definitely know all the clowns who pretend to be messengers but are master illusionists, magicians, covens, practitioners, false prophets, imposters, and impersonators masquerading in a congregation of religious charlatans.

Have you ever asked how a religious group validates their Dharma and faith in God? Shouldn't it be based upon their hours of humanitarian deeds at the end of the journey?

If God does not own a bank account, then where do all the sponsors, memberships, tithes, charities, offerings, donations, scholarships, and blessings for the church really go? Salvation only costs a prayer. One God, one world, one humanity.

Again, a great tip and reminder is that if you use your hotspot as your internet service, it can hack into your own cameras on your television and security systems, so hackers can watch you from your using your cell phone.

It's a crime to block emails or any content coming from your phone. Hacking your workplace's system to steal your information is a crime. Cyber bullying and stalking are crimes.

In the old days, we would choose not to return your call or communicate to you when we didn't want to talk to you. Cyber bullying is a crime against humanity.

When you illegally block someone from receiving thousands of emails, texts, and downloads, hack location details and car computer systems, slow down internet speeds, access cameras in home, block calls, use your phone IP to illegally respond on your behalf, clone your own device, and illegally access a personal information without permission, it is a crime.

Cyber bullying, online stalking, harassment, illegal downloading, identity theft, deletion of data, slowdown of Wi-Fi, blocking access to emails, blocking access to texts, and blocking incoming outgoing calls are all considered illegal surveillance.

Beware that when you use your hotspot on your phone, they can illegally watch you from any cameras inside your home, television, laptops, community cameras, computers, and home security systems.

Dirt Church: Let's talk about an obvious glass ceiling: the bigotry and oppression of women in the Jesuit Catholic faith. Let us remind you that it was a man who was manipulated and tempted Eve to bite the poisonous apple, not the woman. Throughout history, every failed parish man was tested and failed due to their own arrogance, egotism, illusions, betrayals, incompetence, failures, lust, and perversions. They were chasing a hierarchy of clout and status given by the most high God.

This is blatant gender bias, oppression, discrimination, and prejudice. It's the blind leading the blind. Not one woman in this faith is depicted in a positive light of heroism and strength. It feels like a secret society cult of woman haters mandated by the Jesuit Catholic community and elected by their own set of rules.

History has proven that this particular faith has misguided people to believe that they are the only possible hierarchy, but it was built upon the foundation of hypocrites. They throw the rocks, sticks, and stones to hide their own guilt, conspiracy, cloaks, shame, deception, greed, lies, corruption, perversions, gluttony and secularism. This false belief has led many people down the path towards destruction and darkness. Let us remind you that without a woman, there would be no man.

Beware of the wolves in sheep's clothing. Did you know that the Vatican has its very own secret society officers? They are called the Order of the Jesuits. This order was put into place to counter the Protestant reformation that started during the medieval period.

Reformers like President Lincoln, President Kennedy, Malcolm X, Martin Luther King, Jr., and Zwingli began speaking against the teachings of the Jesuits and Roman Catholic Church that were mixed with ritual paganism worship.

Other people who followed this narcissistic leadership included Hitler, who believed the same crazy cruelty, cult doctrine, and philosophies. All of these historical leaders were assassinated for their forthright beliefs. One God, one world, one humanity.

In real time, instant Karma is caught on camera after mocking the anointed chosen ones and divine. Your words, actions, and thoughts create your own reality when instant Karma is served. Remember, Karma is the same exact energy and words you put into reality. The universe does not know when you are joking, and messages get misconstrued in the translations. You manifest the same chaos, defiance, fears, hatred, prayers, anger, and arrogance. These same words mirror back to your reality. It's your manifestation. It is not caused by anyone else's actions. It's your choice of words.

Some of us are such advanced souls that we did not come here to be supported, but we came to be the support system for many. If you've had a challenging life and feel you never had proper support or love, that is because YOU are the love and support.

Do you feel like you bought and settled for the expired counterfeit product instead of buying the real deal Holy Field? Mocking is imitating or making fun of something or someone's behavior or actions in a derisive or contemptuous manner, often to expose their follies, weaknesses, or inconsistencies.

The biggest life lesson is to not ever think it can't happen to you, because unexpected circumstances will happen. The universe does not know when you are joking, so words, thoughts, and emotions are powerful. What you say manifests in your life.

Don't ever judge anyone else for their own choices, because everyone has a different perspective and healing journey that you may not understand.

Mockers will mock, criticizers will criticize, condemners will condemn. Do not take it personally. That is a them problem, not a you problem. Your Karma is how you react, and their Karma is how they treated you. Remember that you will always harvest the seeds that you planted, watered, and sowed.

Don't take the bait. I've smiled in the face of my enemies and know exactly who they are and what they have done to me. Let Gods wrath be the best righteousness. Judgment = Karma.

There are circumstances that will NOT require us to sit with Judas. The Bible does say, "Have nothing to do with them." And then there are circumstances where the Lord will allow a Judas, and it will be really painful. He will ask you to sit at the same table with the person who salted your name, with the one who hurt and betrayed you. It's painful. It's learning to die to your flesh at a very deep level.

Why would the God allow this? We serve God, who takes what the enemy meant for evil and will turn it for good. He will allow it to bring forth the character of Jesus in us. We pray to be more like Jesus. We pray for more of you, Lord, and less of me. So, how do we do this? Romans 12 says that we bless them. We pray for them. We overcome evil with good.

One important part in Romans 12:18 states that if it is possible, as far as it depends on you, live at peace with everyone. It is possible because we can only be responsible for our part to ensure there is peace, and so we do our part to live in peace, and God will take on the rest.

Narcissists deflect attention away from their own behavior, redirecting it onto an innocent party. This ultimately allows them to continue with their exploitative tactics unchecked. The scapegoat becomes burdened with the weight of the narcissist's transgressions, suffering the consequences of being excluded from social circles.

Narcissists manipulate, deceive, and tell lies to weave a web of untruths into a web of deception. Their astute observation skills and keen intuition grant them the insight required to pinpoint the narcissist's true nature. This insight threatens the narcissist's carefully constructed persona, making the scapegoat a dangerous individual who could dismantle their entire façade.

To maintain the position of power and influence, the narcissist skillfully manipulates others into believing that the scapegoat is the instigator of conflict and painted as untrustworthy, emotionally unstable, or even mentally ill. The narcissist successfully tarnishes their reputation and credibility. This ensures that any information or accusations brought forth by the scapegoat are swiftly dismissed or deemed invalid. When you expose the narcissist's manipulation, deception, and lies, it makes them a threat to the narcissist's carefully constructed image. The scapegoat is often shunned.

The words "I am sorry" are the hardest words to say and taste like vinegar going down. For all involved, it's too late. The lies, deceit, and betrayal are too deep. The scars are there to remind you of the lifetimes you healed with the grace of God, from the despair, loneliness, and brokenheartedness. You survived to tell your truth and story. Love yourself more! Stand strong, let go, and let God give them their righteous judgment and Karma.

The day of consequences, reckoning, and redemption is here. Never judge someone based on only a season; be the person that when they get up every morning, the Devil says, "Oh no, she's up!"

Today, I manifest that righteous judgment is given to you, and I let the most high God unleash his wrath. Spiritual and physical sentences await you when God is mocked.

Everything was recorded in the Ethers to ensure righteous judgment is bestowed and served the Ethers court. Today, the wheel of fortune is upright and waiting for justice and Karmic consequences.

The years of unjust harassment, bullying, threats, betrayal, brutality, bribery, cheating, character assassination, perjury, plagiarism, hatred, identity theft, and exploitation to live a lavish lifestyle while toasting on champagne are awaiting untimely destruction. You reap the exact same energy you deserve. Tick tock, Cinderella, the clock has struck midnight, and it's time to give back the lavish lifestyle that you did not deserve.

Surround yourself with the dreamers and the doers, the believers and thinkers, but most of all, surround yourself with those who see greatness within you, even when you don't see it yourself. A little full-moon bathing heals the spirit, wounds, heart, mind, and body and energizes the soul.

Good morning, starshine, the world says hello. Wake up, wake up, you little sleepy angels; it's time to get up and show up. Be grateful for the gifts we have from the universe and the blessings we will continue to receive. You are strong and healed.

Truth and lies are always revealed, especially under every new and full moon. Nothing is ever really hidden. All you have to do is return the negative energy back to the owner and sender. This is not your energy to own; it's their energy

Refute it, rebuke it, transcend it, refuse it, and alchemize the negative energy. Send the negative intentions back to the Ethers for final judgment. This is the same energy you deserve. What you put out is the same energy you receive. Pray to God for protection to close the windows, gates, and doors. Seal them tight, never to open again.

Think about it...this is a very sick way of making you hurt in a place that's extremely vulnerable. Just remember that when dealing with a narcissist, nothing will make sense, and they have no limits on what they will say and do or who they will hurt, including their own children. They'll do whatever gets them what they want, no matter how twisted and obscure that is.

It would seem that the narcissist would lie as an advantage. Sometimes I found that to be true, and yet at other times, my narc would lie for absolutely no reason except to prove that it could be gotten away with. Therapists call this "Duper's Delight." I always said that my own narc could pass a lie detector test since lying came so naturally to him.

Pinocchio had to finally tell the truth and take a lie detector test. I am not the one who was sick, only a little broken from the betrayals. They'd stick a knife in me and twist it, saying, "You know I'd never be unfaithful," when, in fact, I knew otherwise. Think about it...this is a very sick way of making you hurt in a place that's extremely vulnerable.

Just remember that when dealing with a narcissist, nothing will make sense, and they have no limits on what they will say and do, or who they will hurt, including their own children, if it gets them what they want, no matter how twisted and obscure that is.

It would seem that the Narcissist would lie as an advantage. Sometimes I found that to be true, and yet, at other times, my Narc would lie for absolutely no reason except to prove that it could be gotten away with. Therapists call this "Duper's Delight".I always said my own Narc could pass a lie detector test since lying came so naturally that Narcx didn't think anything of it.

People will talk about you when they know they've committed wrongful and negative things toward you. Let them show mercy, forgive them, and let them go for righteous judgment. Remember, do not let anyone's ignorance, hate, drama, or negativity stop you from being the best person you can be. You have control over your destiny.

If you knew how powerful your thoughts, actions, and words were, you would never think a negative thought. The same exact energy you put out is what you receive in return. A booming energy is what you deserve. Karma must be balanced, and you cannot escape from the truth when bad things continues to occur towards you. Karma will affect generations.

People will talk about you when they know they've committed wrongful and negative things toward you. Let them, show them mercy, forgive them, and let go to allow them righteous judgment.

Divine gifts come from above; they cannot be plagiarized, lied about, copied, or stolen. Everyone knows the truth, and most importantly, you cannot hide from God. These guided ideologies and messages did not resonate or originate from you. If you participated in the deception, you will receive the same exact Karma.

Remember, do not let anyone's ignorance, hate, jealousy, envy, drama, or negativity stop you from being the best person you can be. You have control over your destiny.

If you knew how powerful your thoughts, actions, and words were, you would never think a negative thought. The same exact energy you put out is what you receive in return. A booming energy is what you deserve. Karma must be balanced, and you cannot escape from the truth when bad things continue to occur towards you. Karma will affect generations.

Just because you were strong enough for them not to break you doesn't mean you deserved the pain they caused you when you were the innocent victim. Always do what's right in your heart, no matter the consequences, revenge, and retaliation you endured. Everyone was tested, and they failed miserably.

Nobody hates you more than person that can't break you. Never forget that you are made with God's blessings, grace, kindness, love, light, moon, sunshine, star seeds, and a little pixie dust. The evil that they are seeking to do to you, someone is doing it to them. It's their own choices, actions, decisions, and Karma.

This is not shocking news. You were all warned that if you continued to destory the world, you would pay the consequences. History is repeating the same cycles of lessons from the past. It's ridiculous to think that this outdated narrative to divide and conquer actually works, makes sense, or is allowed in the new world order. This belief is a failed system. One God, one humanity, one world.

Now, you all know and realize the only SUPREME SUPER power is the creator of all things. Instead, you spent your time on allowing bullying, lying, degrading, wars, deceit, deception, violence, and self-destruction.

We focused on the motives to destroy humanity, followed false religious teachings, false leaders, cheating, refusal to acknowledge and defend universal laws, refusal to stand up against tyranny, allegiance to secret societies, entitlements, stealing, destruction, greed, racism, prejudice, corruption, hate instead of justice, and the practice of forbearance and solving problems.

The same energy you give out is the same energy you deserved. Everyone is tested on this journey every day. You will receive the same results returning to you. It's a mirrored experience, so start by looking at the man in the mirror. This is your own Karma.

Light workers, thank you for being here on this journey. Because of your hard work, altruistic generosity, godliness, guidance, love, healing wisdom, devotion to compassion, forgiveness, kindness, faith, and reflection, all evil deeds done in darkness will be exposed.

Believe that divine power and Karmic balance will happen on Gaia because of YOU. With so much gratitude, thank you, universe.

We survived to tell the truth. When you find your purpose, you create your own story and do not live for someone else's false narratives, storylines, lies, defamation, and slander. Everyone has a different divine gift, such as music, artistic expression, talent, and messages to guide someone else to see the light in their darkest day. They are grateful to be saved by God and are definitely not a victim.

The lies are always exposed. It is the same exact energy boomeranging and returning to the owner. You cannot hide from Karma like an ostrich in the sand. A reality check is when you realize you were never really hidden from anyone.

Trust and believe in divine timing by allowing yourself permission and consent for righteous judgement to be granted. You're elevating again. This time you're doing it with grace, mercy, love, kindness, and faith. This time, you're doing it with confidence and inner strength. This time, you're doing it with patience and wisdom. You're beginning to realize that letting go allows more blessings to come in.

Raise your head high and your vibes even higher. The Universe is working wonders for you right now. Keep going and healing.

Awaken little sleepers, because the deception will destroy you. So many pastors, influencers, religious leaders, and politicians can't talk about it because they aren't allowed to. They have come into a covenant with these ancient spiritual traditions back from the times of the fallen angels foretold in the Book of Enoch.

We see it manifested in today's "secret societies," and these forces are working to push an agenda and fight against anyone chosen by God to come against these wicked forces. Many have bowed in fear, even though they know the truth.

Some of you need to realize how deep generational curses are and how familiar spirits can be working through you and your family to destroy you. This affects all of us on an individual level, but also as a society. It manifests as righteous Karma.

Do not drink the poisonous Kool-Aid and belief the hype. Not everything is a conspiracy; some of it is truth. Use your brain, common sense, intelligence, and your discernment. A great exposure is coming, so you must choose wisely. Path A leads to an experience of kindness, compassion, abundance, peace, and prosperity. Path B leads you towards chaos, struggle, disappointment, failure, fears, and despair. It is free will, but you are not free from the consequences of your decisions.

Please pick a lie and at least a lane that makes sense. Even humanitarians Joan of Arc, Jesus, Mary Magdaline, Isis, Hawthorn, Martin Luther King, Jr., President Lincoln, President JFK, Neprodite, and Cleopatra were falsely convicted and accused of committing ridiculous crimes of witchcraft, treason, racism, hatred, blasphemy, and conspiracy that were never committed, and they were never proven guilty.

Today, these same tactics are used to segregate people from working together to solve problems. Instead, we use outdated methods of egos, manipulation, tyranny, greed, clout, hidden toxicity, hideous actions, and shameful behaviors.

History repeats itself and has proven that all these statements, stories, and actions were intentional false accusations against innocent leaders who challenged the belief systems and morality of churches, religions, secular governments, outdated systems, and secret societies.

Remember, salvation is free when you repent to the most high God. Your salvation does not cost anything but a prayer. So, if God does not own a bank account, and we leave this world without anything in our possession, then where does all this money go? What if we did not have social media platforms, internet access, electricity, and electronic devices?

While they were judging you, God was developing you. You rose like a phoenix from the ashes. Remember, Karma cannot be transmuted. Be careful of judging people who are experiencing storms right now by adding more rain. No, the storms are not getting worse; they are just getting more obvious.

You can never run away from Karma. There are times where we find ourselves in a vulnerable place, and we don't want to rock the boat in our lives. We don't want to add to the drama going on around us, nor do we want to get involved in situations that will add more stress to our lives. So, we just go with the flow, even if we feel miserable, frustrated, and restless. We don't want to step on anyone's toes or feel any form of rejection, so we just go with it, even when we know it is wrong.

This guilt or any burden you hold onto that is not your own responsibility or burden to carry for others, let it go and forgive yourself. When you bear false witness, knowledge of criminal acts, and falsifying evidence, it only adds to your pain, suffering, and misery. Let them carry their own weight it their poor decisions.

Never judge a book by its cover, and never underestimate anyone. Miracles do come in small packages, like this 10-year-old savant guitarist sharing his gifts with the world. It's just incredible. What have you done to help or share any of your gifts with humanity?

God is ordering your steps and putting you in the right place at the right time. You're not going to be defeated. You're going to make it. Love is without judgment.

"You are completely entitled to opinions that are not supported by evidence. But the moment you spread that opinion as fact, you are a liar. And if you spread it as fact knowing it is not supported by evidence, you are both a liar and a fraud."

Actually, sometimes bad things happen, and it's just awful. You didn't deserve it, and that's the truth. I would rather fall with honesty, integrity, and honor than succeed by being a fraud. You never get away with anything; everything is recorded and documented. Give your permission and consent and allow Karma to be their righteous judgement.

> "Nowadays, people know the price of everything
> and the value of nothing."
> —Olivia Wilde

Don't drink the poisonous Kool-Aid. A soul is just a soul; it does not know about religion, skin color, poverty, greed, belief systems, government, political parties, power, and gender ideology. One world, one God, one humanity.

This is an enemy's secular tactic to divide people from working together. Imagine if we were all blindfolded and put in the same room together. Why would any of this matter?

A bigot is a person who is obstinately or unreasonably attached to a belief, opinion, or faction, especially one that is prejudiced against or antagonistic toward a person or people on the basis of their membership to a particular group.

Everyone prays for a sign from heaven for guidance, clarity, wisdom, and righteous judgment. When you finally have faith, love yourself more, and know your true worth, change happens.

You must sacrifice the things and people who want to tear you apart. No more will you struggle for love. Have the strength to cut those cords. Allow them their own righteous justice and consequences to happen.

Forgive yourself; God already has. Many of us ignored those intuitions, warnings, and red flags. Move aside, and instead let Karma be their catalyst and wrecking ball. Allow God to serve justice, because He can do it better than you could ever imagine. Karma is the same energy you put out and deserve. It's a simple rule in life. If you wouldn't like it done to you, don't do it to others.

Have you ever felt like you were rowing the boat alone, believing you were bailing out the water and navigating others to safety, when you noticed the water inside the boat kept filling up? Then you looked back and realized that the very same people you were sent to help, save, and throw life preservers towards were the very same people putting the holes, filling the boat with rocks, and then hiding their hands the entire time.

Keep rowing through the storms, no matter who is trying to sabotage your survival and successes. Believe that you are never alone, that our miracle-working God does see everything about you and will come to your aid. When you love yourself more, change happens.

I heard your SOS and will always send out the army to try and find you in the middle of darkness to rescue you. Your heart and soul will be measured at the end of the journey. Do not be so angry at others that you miss your own journey. How many times did you leave me alone in the dark to find my own way?

Do not give them power over you. They are blinded by anger and are going to miss their own journey. When we react with visceral anger, we only condemn ourselves. Forgive and let go of people's insults, because they are irreversible and could be catastrophic to yourself.

Do not settle for subpar people in your life. This is your reminder to pick that bar up off that floor. The lesson of this journey is to love yourself more. Your self-worth cannot be measured or destroyed by anyone else.

Decide what kind of life you really want, and then say no to everything that isn't that. Raise the bar up off the floor. You deserve self-respect, kindness, love, loyalty, and trust. Let go, and let righteous judgment prevail.

It seems like everything on Earth is in peril, transition, chaos, destruction, and despair because of the current environment's imbalance. The truth is, the universe uses these towers and storms to cleanse the planet from toxins and impurities.

Our planet continues to use outdated paradigms, patterns, and processes. We can help the world by creating shared environmental resources and building trust and collaboration among relationships in the community.

There are no bank accounts in heaven, and you cannot take possessions with you. If this was the matrix, believe that we are all connected and have the ability to help someone else in this world. Instead, focus on spreading ingenuity, love, peace, joy, light, laughter, and kindness.

Switzerland is not isolated from worldwide realignment. There is a scientific lab focused on creating atmospheric irreversible destruction to our planet. One God, one humanity, one world.

Did the scientists and researchers ever think that by creating a hole in our atmosphere, it could cause irreversible damage to the earth?

Just because we have AI, scientific knowledge, and the ability to split the atom doesn't mean we should. WHO are we really at war with by creating destructive forces against ourselves and the world?

Dirt Church: I am no longer accepting things. I cannot change. I am changing the things I cannot accept. Today is the day for righteous judgement. One day, you will thank yourself for never giving up on yourself.

Scandal is when your own ancestors are embarrassed and abandon you. Respectfully speaking, you never had the power or control. You lost your gifts, power, ranking, status, allegiance, support, credibility, reputation, and spiritual protection because of the way you've treated others.

Manipulation is when they always blame you for reacting to their toxic behavior but don't discuss their disrespect that triggered you.

You can stretch me of everything I have; I will walk away and go get it again. It's in me. When there is an unhealthy connection, it's perfectly okay to outgrow it and walk away. If that connection is unhealthy, it's more than okay to outgrow it.

Someday, we will forget the hurt and the reason we cried and who caused us pain. We will finally realize that the secret of being free is not revenge, but letting things unfold in their own way and their own divine timing. After all, what matters is not the first but the last chapter of our life, which shows us how we ran the race.

Remember, when people seek revenge, strong people forget them, and intelligent people ignore their behavior. You never look good making someone else look bad.

Make sure you are not drinking from the wrong pitcher. The only authority anyone has over you is what you gave to them. Remember, never regret walking away from any negative toxicity you have outgrown which does not serve your higher purpose. This is courageous. Let go, and let Karma be their own wrath.

Bringing to light all the evidence, schemes, backstabbing, stalking, bullying, persecution, privacy, HIPPA violations, hacking, illegal surveillance, identity fraud, betrayals, thievery, stealing property, lies, blocking access to work, plagiarism, shadow banning, false reporting, accusations, paying bribes, online harassment, and threats against me.

The truth was that through years of misery and abuse you finally survived by walking away and deciding that enough was enough. Instead, they sought revenge.

The Watchman Never Give Up:
The Truth Is Always Revealed and Exposed

I can never understand how the victim of the abuser who committed the crimes and attacks became targeted because of the lies they told. Then the victim is targeted again after exposing their deception and lies when speaking their truth.

Those entities and attachments are real…there's a lot behind a person who is pretending to be fine! Use your discernment…

When you refuse to be manipulated or fooled by their ridiculous narrative, antics, lies, behavior, or actions, they will always try to tell people you were just hard to deal with or crazy.

Sometimes, people think they have done something right behind your back that can hurt you. Remember, nothing is hidden from God's eyes. Absolutely every action, good or bad, is seen by Him. This thought can bring comfort and strength in knowing that God is aware of everything.

When you feel betrayed or hurt by someone's actions, trust that God will bring righteous justice and healing. Keep your faith strong and continue to act with kindness and integrity, because God rewards those who remain faithful and righteous.

The moment Judas accepted the bribe, the coin touched his hand, and the blood money was received for the betrayal of Jesus. This sacriicer changed history forever and led to Jesus's demise.

The guilt triggered Judas. He knew he had caused treason, blasphemy, and lies, and he tried to return the money, but it was too late. Judas's entire lineage is known for being traitors. Judas did not last much longer.

The guilt made him mentally suffer because of his betrayal. Righteous judgment is handed down the moment you accept the betrayal. Your judgment and fate are sealed when you accepted the sacrifice. You reap the same seeds you sow.

Cut the cords to anyone who no longer serves your higher purpose. You can't get out of debt while keeping the same lifestyle that got you there. Cut out everything except the basics.

My, what big eyes you have, the better to see you with my dear! My what a big mouth you have, the better to deceive and lie to you my dear! My what beautiful clothes you are wearing, the better to cloak myself my dear! My what big teeth you have, the better to devour and trap you my dear!

We are among wolves in sheep's clothing, and many are being deceived and led down the wrong path with false narratives, false beliefs, false promises, false teachings, false prophets, and false light!

I was falling for it myself until the flock opened their eyes to see and ears to hear the truth. Use your own common sense and discernment.

Sometimes, you really need to open your eyes and see what people show you, not just the good you want to see. I am thankful, grateful, and blessed to learn from these lessons. When you claim your power back and the parts stolen from you is when your healing process begins. Give yourself permission and consent to forgive others. Manifestations start with pure intentions, happiness, from a place of love, and from a healed heart.

The truth is revealed eventually in the right time, at the right door, and for the right opportunity. Just show up and do your part, then let Him handle the rest. You should protect yourself by choosing who is allowed in your energy.

Mary, Mary, quite contrary, how does your garden grow? Where did you plant your seeds? What garden did you grow and water?

Better to admit that you walk through the wrong door then spend your life in the wrong room. We can't always choose the music we dance to in our life, but we can choose who we dance with.

Sometimes, you just have to let go and let God serve righteous judgment. He can hit harder than you ever could. Karma must be balanced by the universe. The truth is always revealed in divine timing.

Atrocities are when you finally understand you were all tested and given enough rope to truly hang yourselves. The "aha" moment is when all of your deceit, slander, false testimony, character assassination, toxic behavior, bearing false witness, plagiarism, theft, identity theft, bullying, stalking, harassment, technical data breaches, HIPPA violations, unlawful surveillance, retaliation, revenge, and lies are revealed. You never had power over anyone.

The question is, how far did our judiciary system go to protect the criminals and corruption instead of protecting the victims? Did anyone ever seek the truth from the victims?

Bravo, here is a hero who is doing the right thing regardless of status, clout, title, ranking, money, and position. When you broke the law or did something legal, you deserved the consequences.

A liar's worst enemy is someone with a good memory, someone who is detail-oriented, retains their integrity by empathetic record keeping of signed contracts and agreements, loan payoffs, real estate transactions, and recorded evidence, like voice mails, emails, texts, bank statements, phone records, grievances filed, computer data, and years of performance paperwork collected. Just be honest, it's not that difficult.

Tell the truth in the beginning, because it will always come to light. When you destroy someone's life with lies, take it as a loan; it will come back to you with interest.

You can't control anyone else's actions, and loyalty comes from the heart. You are never a victim, and your character is developed by your own narrative. How it ends is up to you.

Never lose your faith. Follow your soul, not the crowd. Make decisions that reflect your values, virtues, and integrity, rather than making decisions out of fear of judgment, shame, or guilt. Stay true to who you are rather than seeking approval or validation from anyone outside yourself.

Follow your guiding light, your North Star. Break out of the box of society's standards and limited beliefs. Lead with love, light, forgiveness, and grace. Keep being your beautiful authentic self. You are eternally loved, blessed, and precious.

Nobody can steal your destiny from you or take your royal crown. This light of mine, I'm gonna let it shine, let it shine, let it shine!

IN CASE YOU FORGOT:

1. You are a soul/spirit/universe wearing a human mask.

2. You are here to remember who you are and help humanity.

3. What you love is the key to your purpose.

4. Your challenges are meant to trigger your growth.

5. There are no mistakes, only lessons.

6. You are so much more than what society wants you to believe.

7. Love is the greatest medicine and healing you will ever experience.

8. Love and Light is who we are.

9. Find pure joy and happiness, and practice self-love.

10. Guilt and fear

11. Plant your own seeds and water your garden to grow amazing plants.

12. Let's wake up and remember who we are.

Yep, all 10 solar lights turned on when I stood next to them all at the same time. This happens to me often, but just as a reminder you have the power. This little light of mine, I'm gonna let it shine, this little light of mine, I'm gonna let it shine, let it shine, let it shine, let it shine!

Believe in miracles—I am opening doors for you. I will close the doors that you do not need to go through. I will lead the way, so follow my lead. I will restore all that you have lost and give you days filled with my grace and blessings.

Until you take accountability for your own actions, truly change your behavior and outdated beliefs, trust in faith, elevate your soul, and learn the lessons of Karma, it will continue to happen lifetime after lifetime. It's within us to seek justice for injustices. Just forgive, let it go, and let righteous judgment happen.

It's within someone's destiny to speak the truth. There have been lies. It's your destiny to bring balance and do things that have been unbalanced. Always remember that you have power over your destiny, and no matter what storms may come your way, you will fulfill it lifetime after lifetime! My grace is being heavily rewarded.

Some people are angry, annoyed, mad, and upset at you because you are not suffering the way they expected you to. May God keep on disappointing them. Karma will bring you divine righteous justice. Forgiveness is for your own healing. Let it all go!

Karmic and universal laws must be applied. Just because it's taking time doesn't mean it's not happening.

Sometimes the people you would give your life for will not care about you. Sometimes the people you openly defend in public are the same ones trying to destroy your character in private.

It's a difficult truth, but it's one that opens your eyes to one of the realest lessons you will come to learn: you don't always get what you give.

Imagine having the love of someone who literally put a shield of protection around you who has manifested and divined on your behalf in ways tangible to you, who nurtures you in all realms, and who supports you in all realms. Now imagine being dumb enough to fumble the bag.

These past few years have pushed me to love and take care of myself more. There is nothing I enjoy more than minding my own business, finding new ways to grow, and thriving in silence. You say it's antisocial. I say it's prayer for peace.

Spend time with loved ones who appreciate the beauty of life and of the world instead of following false narratives. We need to remember to ignore ignorance and not to volunteer for stupidity. We cannot control others' reactions; we can only control and change ourselves.

Many of us spent our entire life wearing masks to fit in with clout-chasing society by pretending to believe in their ideals, their religions, their immorality, their choices, their values, and their world instead of learning, growing, healing, and leading others to the truth.

Instead, we cared more about popular culture, social media platforms, and creating content of false images. We aligned with the popular trends and influencers who expected us to be true followers for the purpose of self-promotion and greed. We never stopped to think about the morality or the parts that did not fit with other people's expectation.

> I release all that which brings me pain, anxiety, and fears.
> I release all that which blocks my growth.
> I release all that which is blocking love from my life.
> I release all that which is toxic within me and around me.
> I release each and every thing that is not in alignment with my divinity.

A wise man makes his own decisions; an ignorant man follows the public opinion. Ignorance is when you reject something you don't even understand or really know anything about.

Arrogance, manipulation, criticism, toxic behavior, cruelty, delusion, deflection, stupidity, and ignorance are the armor worn by a group of narcissistic cowards and master gaslighting illusionists.

When you develop your true nature, you navigate through the stormy seas. These storms were made to build up your confidence to tell your narrative. Always trust and follow your intuition.

You can't save everyone; some people are going to destroy themselves no matter how much you help them. Don't destroy yourself trying to help the helpless. No matter the weapon formed against you, it will ever prosper.

The Devil is so confused about how you are still standing after every weapon was thrown at you to destroy you by your enemies. You did not break Every wicked weapon thrown bounced right back towards them to destroy and burden them, not you.

You did not break. You bent a little, but you did not break. Stand in your power, truth, and faith to rebuke, refute, return, transmute, transcend, and alchemize any negative energy, and you will never fail. No one has more power over you than the mighty God. Allow permission and consent for righteous judgment to be granted. Pull back 100% of your power and energy. You are still standing.

The best part of being authentic is that there is no image to maintain. You will delight some and disturb others, and none of it will concern the truth of your being.

> Don't talk about it—be about it. Stop wishing—start doing!
> Keep speaking your truth
> Keep doing you
> Keep healing
> Keep smiling
> Keep evolving
> Keep enjoying your peace and love
> Keep encouraging love, peace, and light to return.
> All negative energy returns back to sender, known or unknown, ten thousand times over
> Believe it, speak it, claim it, and so shall it be.

It's glorious to finally realize that you had the power within you the entire time. Stay focused on faith, trust, evolving, learning, growing, and healing. Know your self-worth, and set clear boundaries to protect your peace and energy.

We are in weird times right now...the best thing to do is love who loves you and protect your energy. Believe in yourself, because the cheat code to life is the power within you.

You cannot reverse what you have sent out; it's the same energy you deserve. It is during the worst storms of your life that you will get to see the true colors of the people you thought cared for you. It's all in illusion. You don't have trust issues, you have learned a life lesson, and you are not making that mistake again.

You're a one-hit wonder, stealing other people's creative content and ideas that are obviously not your own. You didn't think this was a crime to steal from someone else? It's against universal laws and God's law to steal, commit crimes against morality, steal content, assassinate character, and stalk to plagiarize someone else's creative expression, inspiration, and ideas that came directly from Him.

Did you really think that you could fake out God? It's absolutely, ridiculous and outrageous, because every creative cell comes from the divine. There are no shortcuts in this life; you must do the work. Every position of power, title, and ranking are given to those who are divinely devoted to him. If you participated, then you will receive the same divine righteous judgment and consequences.

It's like stealing Moses's ten commandments from his own house or plagiarizing the Bible from the works of the disciples and calling it your own creation. It's blasphemy, treason, and hypocrisy to the highest realms to call any of this creative work your own when you were never given this calling, power of inspiration, divine downloads, intuitive knowledge, or intellectual property granted by God or the universe.

You cannot plagiarize, steal, or cheat your way into the kingdom.

Always have a plan B. There was always a higher plan for you. All of the hard work, challenges, complicated decisions, and difficult times were preparing you for what's next. You were always enough.

You are filled with incredible ABILITIES and the POWER to accomplish what you want. Your energy is a powerful FORCE and catalyst for change. Get ready for the season of blessings and miracles.

Tyrants are unfit to be the rulers of the world of free people and are not the real problem. It's the people who obey tyrants. Regardless, it's all an illusion, because the people have true power and always have.

Sometimes God takes you on a new adventure and journey you didn't know you needed to bring you everything you ever wanted.

It was meant in this lifetime to break all family generational curses because it stops with you. Many were tested and failed. The things you are passionate about are not random. They are your calling and divine purpose.

May everything that you want and need align for you. Be your true self. The light always shines through the darkness. Your intuition is a divine gift, so embrace it.

The worst person is someone who is two-faced. They wear masks and masquerade in front of others as morally superior citizens, but the reality is that this group is paid to spread venomous hatred and lies by gossiping to gain sympathy from one group of people, and then they will spread slander to another group to destroy their reputation.

Some of you are wearing a mask to church, but you've been doing it for years, masquerading as knowing God while judging other's religion, faith, and beliefs when they are the ones who lack morality. Solve the problem or leave the problem, but don't live with the problem.

Be very careful of the words you speak, because they become your reality. It's such a compliment when someone says you look so much happier. Some of you are mad about wearing a mask to church, but you've been doing it for years while mocking other's beliefs, faith, and religion.

Things hidden deep within come back. Everything always comes back, especially the things that you didn't think about, have not overcome, ignored, dealt with, or healed from. They will hit you out of the blue one day and tap you on the shoulder to say, "Remember me?"

Stop trying to recycle the things that the universe is trying to replace. You're making whoever doubted you believe in divine favor over your life. One day, you will tell your story of how you overcame what you went through, and it will be someone else's survival guide. Be the narrator of your own survival success and journey.

Consider how precious your soul must be when God and the Devil are fighting over it. One day, I tried to throw in the towel. God threw it right back and said, "Wipe your tears, get back up, and fight, because you are almost there." Trust in HimHe will always have your back and fight in your corner.

We are never alone; love and light are always with us. Focus on bringing unity to your community.

> Dear Universe,
>
> Thank you for allowing other like-minded souls to cross my path. As more of us merge together into a soul family and soul tribe, the stronger our bridge becomes. I'm thankful for both those who I can inspire and those who inspire me.
>
> In our small community, there are 2000 homeless people every night. The shelters only hold 300 people. Recently, a church did volunteer to shelter them but was denied by the local authority government agency and neighborhood councils.
>
> What if we used the abandoned company factories, properties, churches, airports, Colosseums, schools, commercial buildings, public buildings, and parks to create housing for the homeless?
>
> If God's salvation is free, He does not own a bank account, and we can't take anything to the kingdom with us, then where do the church's money, tithes, offerings, donations, charitable contributions, and scholarships really go?

In *Ripley's Believe It or Not,* the Truth Always Comes Out

"Someone feels like you're exploiting them because you keep exposing things they've done to you. If you are speaking out online, its a group of haters who are involved in a hater group of individuals hiding behind their own community's corruption. They're wearing masks of immortality to cover their illegal deeds, and their fake pages are reporting your profile and your posts to block your own work. This is their pathetic attempt to try and silence you to steal content for their profit. A secret society paid people to destroy and stalk you because you spoke out as a truth speaker and whistleblower against them, causing undue havic, destruction, and harassment, claiming you are just attention-seeking because you are exposing them. They are also leaving comments to try to get under your skin. They have direct ties to social media platform agents and hackers who were paid to make changes and block you."

"If they didn't want to be exposed, they shouldn't have been doing dumb shit, especially to you."

The Watchmen

Disrespect will close doors that apologies can't open! Be careful how you treat people you think you don't need! They don't lie to you, because the truth will hurt your feelings. They lie to you, because the truth might provoke you to make the choices that won't serve their own interest.

Emotional intelligence doesn't come with age; it comes with experience. Be very careful of the toes you stomp on today, because they can be connected to the derrière you have to kiss tomorrow.

People who get excited about the moon and stars every night, speak from the heart, stay in the car to listen to music a little bit longer, and are kind for no reason are my kind of people.

The matrix is about how well you learned and applied the principles, techniques, skills, and lessons learned while passing through the game levels and challenges set within by the masters. Find the glitch.

Sometimes there is not a reset button, game credit, or bonus point earned to buy another life.

Never give another person the chance, opportunity, or lifetime to waste your valuable time. Be grateful you learned your self-worth and love from the failures and mistakes and grew from the lessons.

Let them talk, because it will only bless you more when you are innocent. People like being in your Kool-Aid even when they don't even know the flavor. Eat the meat and spit out the bones. Don't be an easily led target by a group of hateful people.

It is shameful to blame others for their own scandalous Jezebel actions and behaviors when it's your party lifestyle that caught you up! It's blasphemous and ridiculous, because a divine is protected, disciplined, celibate, and disease-free. These conditions are your Karmic righteous judgment for the lies and shameless fodder you told to others.

I've seen the Vatican in Rome, where masses celebrated and cheered at a glimpse of the Pope. These followers idolize this man as a higher level of power and revered figure of faith, saint, angel, emperor, king, God, and Jesus. He seems to be a man who is wearing the Emperor's clothing.

Why do we identify with false profits who cannot provide salvation of a soul into the kingdom of heaven? Who does not hold supreme authority to the kingdom? Who does not hold the power of God, Jesus, Kings, or Emperors? Who cannot heal anyone from illness or sickness? Who cannot protect anyone from death? It's ridiculous that people will conceal and control the image of the true leader of the kingdom.

Trauma teaches you to close your heart and armor up. Healing teaches you to open your heart and boundaries up. A woman who has healed from multiple traumatic experiences on her own and still keeps her heart pure is an alchemist. At the end of this journey, the right people will fight for you, not against you. The right people will show up.. The right people will show you love, light, and kindness. You became who you needed to be in order to survive. But now it's time to become who you need to be so you can thrive in life. Change is coming. It's time to embrace it.

What seeds did you plant in your garden? Did you water the trees with positive energy, love, kindness, light, and healing? Remember, you will reap exactly what seeds you have sown. There is a reason why everything feels so chaotic right now. This time on earth has been prophesied and predicted for millennia.

Many believed it was coming for years. It is not the end of times —it's the birth of a new era, new generation, new world order. We were given lifetimes to grow our own legacy and garden. One God, one world, one humanity.

God wants you to pay attention to the spirit of offense attacking you through people. You are not crazy, and your discernment is correct. God loves you enough to show you when someone is not for you, so pay attention to the signs He has been showing you. Let the towers fall down in their lives to allow righteous judgment. God's wrath will prevail, as will universal balance and Karma.

Tyrants and bullies do not have the right to take your peace away from you. The reality is, it's their own anger projected onto you for the failures of their own life. It's a mirror image of shame, ignorance, and disappointment, and it is exactly what they have given to others.

Forgive the tyrant and bully, because they Great advice, tyrants and bully's do not have the right to take your peace away from you. Reality, it's their own anger projected onto you for the failures of their own life. It's a mirror image of shame, ignorance, disappointment and is exactly what they have given to others.

Forgive the tyrant and bully, because they may have not healed from their own childhood trauma and wounding. This is a them problem, not a you problem. You are not a product of your environment, and you have total control of the decisions made in your own life. Stand up for what is right. If you know about it, talk about it.

A breach of contract is against criminal law. Never control them. Let them do what they're going to do so you can see what they would rather do. Their actions will show you how much they respect you.

CRIMINAL LAW CONDITION OF TERMS

CRIMINAL LAW is that branch or division of law which defines crimes, treats of their nature, and provides for their punishment.

CRIME: Crime is defined as an act committed in violation of public law forbidding or commanding it.

GENERAL (characteristic of criminal law)—general, in that criminal law is binding on all persons who live.

TERRITORIAL (characteristic of criminal law)—in that criminal law undertakes to punish crimes committed within Philippine territory.

PROSPECTIVE (characteristic of criminal law)—in that a law cannot make an act punishable in a manner in which was not punishable when committed.

Your angel is saying to you, "Stay strong and believe in miracles." Your blessings are coming; claim them today through faith. The thing about working hard consistently is that you don't see the results for a long time, then you see all the results at once. Success is a process, and the ones who stay on the path come out on top.

Do not be a hater. Release all bitterness, anger, malice, malicious slander, judgment, hatred, ungodliness, and unrighteousness behavior towards others. You will suffer the same consequences.

Does anyone actually think this system makes sense? The good news is that we are on the verge of a major victory to fix the broken Electoral College system by convincing Michigan to join the National Popular Vote Interstate Compact, a nonpartisan effort to replace the current Electoral College system with a legal agreement among the states to award their electoral votes to the winner of the national popular vote.

Will you send the Electoral College system to the trash bin of history? Let's get this done! Under the current Electoral College system, candidates spend almost all their time campaigning in just a handful of swing states.

Some people will learn how to appreciate you by losing you. Go where you are celebrated, not tolerated. If people treat you like an option, leave them like a choice. You're worth being loved and valued.

Set boundaries against your haters. If God is your boss, then what crazy enemy would ever attack you? You can never hide from the truth or facts. Every action is recorded to ensure righteous judgment, and Karma is rewarded. You cannot undo past wrongdoings, but you can change the course of the future.

For your own sanity, let things be. You will feel easier when you don't always think about it, so for your sanity, let things be. Don't control it, roll with it. What flows, flows. What crashes, crashes. It is what it is.

If standing up for yourself burns bridges, then I have matches, and we ride at dawn. When the truth shines, it's like turning on the lights and exposing all the cockroaches as they run for cover from their wrongdoings. Always stand up for your truth.

There's something very wrong with your spirit if you get pleasure from spreading hatred, tyranny, evil thoughts, ego, arrogance, envy, jealousy, secrecy, bullying, slander, threats, bigotry, racism, harassment, lying, humiliating, embarrassing, and belittling other people.

Stand back and let God handle it, because he sees it, too. There is no escaping the universe's truth. The fact is, they never got away with anything, and it only exposed them even more than their crimes.

Give permission and consent to serve righteous judgment on your behalf. Vengeance is God's wrath, not yours. All you need to do is forgive, do better when you know better, and begin the healing process within by loving yourself more.

The enemy is going to try to knock you down, but he will not succeed. It's only a test. Some of you will pass, and some of you will fail the exam even with an open book. Pay more attention to people's intentions and mindset rather than their appearances. Don't confuse the soul with the shell. The Devil is a great liar.

When you love someone, you protect them from the pain, you don't become the cause of it. Your relationship is with God, not religion. An empress is hard to find, easy to lose, and impossible to replace. Change is scary, but so is staying the same. When you feel a fear of changing or staying stuck, be fearless.

God will put you back together in front of those who broke you. All the pressure they put you through only made you stronger and into a brilliant, unbreakable, flawless diamond. Never give up love, be fearless, practice unconditional faith, and most of all, be grateful.

We could spend our whole lives waiting for someone to apologize or take responsibility for how they hurt us before we decide to let go. But the problem with that scenario is, we've made someone else in charge of how and when we heal.

If we truly want to break a cycle and heal, we have to forget about what the other person is or isn't doing and focus entirely on our own process. Violence starts with dehumanizing language or taking accountability for their actions, hate crimes, and domestic terrorism.

Spread peace, not wars and violence. Spread creativity, not destruction. Spread empathy, not hate. Spread generosity, not greed. One world , one God, one humanity.

Let Your Light Shine to the Heavens, Universe, and Earth

He says, "Be still, and know that I am God; i will be exalted among the nations, I will be exalted in the earth."

Psalms 46:10

I broke the chains that were binding me, healed my heart and broken pieces, and cut the cords from my childhood wounds and intolerable memories.

What do you owe yourself? For starters, you owe yourself forgiveness for all the unnecessary hardships.

Learn from every mistake and experience. Some people have been some additional courses you could've done without.

You owe yourself a lot more moments of peace to balance out all the moments you worried about.

You owe yourself the ability to not only dream big, but to manifest big.

You owe yourself space to sit with your emotions and allow them to seep through you until they've been resolved.

You owe it to yourself to harness your strengths. What do you owe yourself? Ask yourself if anything else can be manifested, and let it be what you deserve from yourself first. You are worthy of it all.

Not everyone will understand your journey. That's fine. It's not their journey to make sense of, it's yours. Remember, the spiritual journey can be arduous, as it often involves unlearning societal conditioning, questioning established belief systems, and seeking answers beyond the continues of conventional wisdom.

Remember, you are not alone, and you have a mission, a purpose. Keep shining, keep growing, and keep spreading your love and light throughout the world!

Breaking Generational Curses

One of the significant tasks to undertake is to break free from the chains of generational curses. These curses are patterns of negative energy, beliefs, or behaviors that have been passed down through ancestral lineage. It's not an easy task, but by doing so, they pave the way for future generations to experience a life free from the burdens of the past.

Healing Karma Across Lifetimes

We are on a mission to heal not only the Karma of our current lives, but also the Karma accumulated throughout our past incarnations. We carry within us the weight of unresolved energies and lessons from previous lifetimes. By consciously addressing and healing this Karmic debt, we create an opportunity for personal growth, transformation, and collective healing.

Breaking Free from the Matrix

You must liberate yourself from illusions and limitations of the matrix. The matrix represents the societal and cultural constructs that often confine individuals, preventing them from recognizing their true divine nature. Breaking free from conformity allows you to transcend to discover your authentic self.

This pursuit of freedom can sometimes clash with societal norms, leading to a sense of isolation and the feeling of being misunderstood. Don't worry if others like you or not; most people don't even like themselves. It doesn't matter how dirty others play; Karma has a big bite. Always move with a genuine heart and pure intentions. You can never run or hide from Karma; it knows your address.

Storms in our lives create towers and forces of trajectory to clear the path of objects so we can move forward. Your decisions are your responsibility and fate.

Learn the difference between connection and attachment. Remember, some people are here to teach you a lesson and are here for only a season. Do not become too attached; let it flow.

Connections versus Attachments

> Connection gives you power, while attachment sucks the life out of you.
> Connection is love. Attachment is obsession.
> Connection gives you choice. Attachment is control.
> Connection leads to empowerment. Attachment leads to imprisonment.
> A connected person draws energy from within (from the divine).
> An attached person pulls energy from without (from others).
> Connection builds wealth. Attachment breeds poverty.

You don't know what others are going through or how many times they have fallen down and gotten back up again! There's a story behind everyone. There's a reason why they are the way they are. Think about that and don't judge.

Plagiarism is the theft of someone else's original content and work efforts and selling them as your own idea or original content. In most countries, copyright is a legal right that protects original works of authorship.

Typically, if you create an original work, you have a copyright from the moment you create the original idea. If the original idea was not yours, you are in violation. Visual or audiovisual works include the folowing: videos, movies, TV shows and broadcasts, video games, paintings, and photographs. Audio works include the folowing: songs, musical compositions, sound recordings, and spoken word recordings. Written works include the following: books, plays, manuscripts, articles, and musical scores.

Please note, only an original work is eligible for copyright protection. To be original enough for copyright protection, a work needs to be created by the author themselves and have some minimal amount of creativity. Generally, names, titles, slogans, or short phrases aren't considered to be original enough to qualify for copyright protection.

Copyright generally doesn't protect facts or ideas, but it may protect the original words or images that express a fact or idea. This means that you may be able to express the same idea or fact as another author, as long as you don't copy that author's way of expressing that idea.

Have more respect for genuine people. They may not be perfect, but at least they're real. Keep going. Don't stop now, you're almost at the finish line.

Your originality shines through and cannot be copyrighted, plagiarized, fabricated, or by faked. Please note, only an original work is eligible for copyright protection. To be original enough for copyright protection, a work needs to be created by the author themselves and have some minimal amount of creativity.

Generally, names, titles, slogans, or short phrases aren't considered to be original enough to qualify for copyright protection. For example, the symbol "+" is likely not subject to copyright, but a painting full of shapes and colors arranged in a unique pattern is likely protected.

May everything that's good, positive, healthy, and soul-nourishing find its way to you. Let your soul shine brightly. Don't let others' deceit to block your path and destiny in order to hide their diabolical wrongdoing and actions against you. They want to dim your shine.

Your soul's shine and authenticity cannot be copied or duplicated by anyone.

Virtue is the character of a moral behavior showing high moral standards. A paragon of virtue is a quality considered morally good or desirable in a person. Patience is a virtue.

Having integrity is a good or useful quality. There's no virtue in suffering in silence.

There is no escape hatch, parachute, or avoiding towers when righteous judgment is applied. Karma is served individually based on your own actions and participation in the deception.

The enemy continues to attack, block, steal, plagiarize, commit fraud, thievery, and destruction, cause misguided communication and false leadership, and steal intellectual property because of their own actions of greed.

The higher purpose of the divine messages are to guide people to the salvation of their own souls. Many people are so lost in their own self imprisonment, hate, bigotry, jealousy, envy, bullying, bitterness, shame, hurt, addictions, mental health issues, malice, greed, peril, oppression, pain, sorrow, grief, brokenness, and darkness that they cannot see the way to the light to heal from trauma.

Have faith that this is the season of restoration. Restoration is the action of returning something to a former owner. All that was stolen will be returned to you seven times over. Remember, every step and action counts in climbing the stairway to heaven.

Acting too much in your own ego, arrogance, and pride will eventually result in shame. Pride is the feeling of deep pleasure or satisfaction derived from one's own achievements, the achievements of those with whom one is closely associated, or qualities or possessions that are widely admired.

Copyright infringement is the unauthorized and unlawful usage of a copyrighted work. Copyright infringement is the use of works protected by copyright without permission for a usage where such permission is required, thereby infringing certain exclusive rights granted to the copyright holder, such as the right to reproduce, distribute, display, or perform the protected work, or to produce derivative works.

I have proof of a 200-page book started in 2018. There are 168 Instagram influencers who committed crimes of thievery, perjury, fraud, and plagiarism, and I can prove it. Every post is dated, and time stamped. I can prove it in court, can you?

These spiritual teachings were free to help heal the world, but instead you chose to steal the content to claim it was your original content and idea for your own greed, All you cared about was becoming the next famous motivational influencer for status and clout. Now all the stolen content is on the platform, and you are receiving proceeds from my stolen content that you did not have my permission to copy. I am giving you one day's notice to remove all plagiarism, perjury, fraud, and copyright infringement violations your company has committed. You earned all of your proceeds from my stolen unauthorized intellectual property. These divine teaching were free to the world; however, your misaligned counterfeit leadership messages and fraudulent guidance for greed, status, fame, and clout. All fraudulent copyright content stolen from my platforms must be removed and payment remitted to me within 48 hours.

Terms:

1. Remove all plagiarized and stolen intellectual property violations and posts within 48 hours from all social media platforms.
2. To prevent further criminal prosecution, refund the entire portfolio from unauthorized stolen intellectual property. This includes alll revenues over seven years.

We literally crack up to see how fast the online stalkers will commit the copyright infringement crimes. Within minutes of the divine downloaded message being posted, the message is electronically sent to the community.

The Instagram page has an option to report and remove intellectual property theft. Instagram is aware and tracking; however, within minutes there are hundreds of illegal copyright infringement infractions and copyright violation cases. This proves my point that there is online stalking, harassment, and bullying occurring. For five years, I can prove it an electronic format and timestamp every post in journal and book format. I was asked to prove the book and journal were mine. It's 200 pages.

The individuals who truly work on themselves, who sit in silence with their own humanity and reverse engineer themselves back to their core essence, are the leaders of the new era. We defy averages and statistics because our journey is wildly misunderstood.

Unfortunately, when you thought about it, participated in it, joined and laughed about it, knew about it, and avoided doing anything about it, you were as guilty as the rest of the corrupt criminals.

Karma will boomerang right back to you 10 times over. You can never avoid the towers of Karma. The truth will set you free. Universal law and Karma must be balanced.

Contempt is the feeling that someone is lacking skills, is beneath you for consideration, is worthless, provides negative counsel to disregard someone else's opportunities, and advises others to block you and not consider you worthy of consideration. These people disregard you out of blind jealousy and blatant envy.

This is clearly bigotry, or hatred occluded by a misguided mindset. The only way into the kingdom is through the creator, not through anyone else. The crazy thing about people who don't like you is that they watch everything you do. When you finally know, enough is enough.

Trust your intuition. You don't need to explain or justify your feelings to anyone. Just trust your own inner guidance, it knows best. God will prove the haters wrong.

We have created a society that feels it's okay to steal someone else's intellectual creative content and claim it as their own original work. Their entire existence is to become the next up-and-coming generational influencer. No one asked if this was okay.

It's never okay to steal or cheat your way into heaven. You cannot copy someone else's work and claim it as your personal work without permission from the creator. These motivational quotes are from my personal life experiences and stories, not yours. Yes, this easily proven in my journal and book. See you in court.

Never blame anyone else but yourself for your own mistakes, life choices, and decisions. You must take ownership and responsibility to tell the truth. Assigning blame to others to cover up the mistakes you did is wrong.

> Good people give you happiness.
> Bad people give you experience.
> Worst people give you lessons.
> Best people give you memories

Deflection is when every time you wanted to address something that bothered you, you became the problem. You can't blame God for your own actions on your journey and must take accountability. Whatever seems to trigger you is the problem mirrored back to you of what you really need to heal.

We all have the ability to choose the path to practice disinterest and selfless concern for the well-being of others. The world can use a reminder to work towards true altruism. We need to let go of outdated capitalism and segregated beliefs that are not in alignment with humanity's ideology.

> "Every man must decide whether he will walk in the light of creative altruism or in the darkness of destructive selfishness."
> —Martin Luther King, Jr.

What legacy are you going to leave behind for the next generation? I wish world peace, hope, love, and a little pixie dust! Remember, without the darkness, we will never see the beautiful stars.

All narcissists are hypocrites. They pretend to have integrity, morals, and values that they really don't possess. Behind closed doors, they lie, insult, criticize, disrespect, and abuse.

They can do and say whatever they want, but how dare you say anything back to them or criticize them. They have a whole set of rules for others but follow none of their own rules and practice nothing of what they preach.

You are never the product of your environment and can choose how you treat others. Forgiveness is for your own healing and is necessary to test your ability to heal from trauma.

Don't blame a clown for following another clown. Ask yourself why you continue to buy the ticket and go to the circus.

Sometimes we feel like a caged bird, and we cannot free ourselves, even when the cage door is open. It's because we forgot the feeling of freedom due to conditioned forms of abuse we experienced as childhood trauma.

When we finally realize that freedom comes from within ourselves and has the power and ability to free ourselves from self-imprisonment, we can open that cage door anytime and fly to freedom, or we can chose to stay caged in fear inside.

Abuse is a bad effect or for a bad purpose or misuse: the judge abused his power to treat others with cruelty. Abuse includes violence, assault, and speaking offensive insults. Abuse is never normal, and this uncontrolled behavior is never okay. Abuse is never okay. It's patterned childhood conditions, and it's never okay.

You are never the product of your own environment. You have the ability to choose to change how you treat and forgive others. This step is the very first step to the healing process.

Your character will outweigh any lie told about you; remember that. Those who know you, know you. It's good to have people in your life who love you for you, people who see, encourage, and support the best in you. If someone wants to be slanderous, let them. If someone wants to believe their lies, let them. If someone wants to create and or get involved in drama, let them. Your life is a precious gift; your time is too valuable to be bothered with such silliness.

You cannot control what people think, say, or do, but you can control how you respond. God reads our thoughts, hears our words, and sees our deeds, and remember, we will each one day stand before Him and give an account to Him (Romans 14:12). So don't let what someone else thinks, says, or does be your excuse for responding in a like manner.

Prescribe the worlds realty. Arrogan, eris having excessi, best pride in oneself often contempt for others. Greed is an intense and selfish desire for scheming things, especially prosperity or fraud. Fraud is the wrongful or criminal deception intended to result in selfish financial or personal gains. A fraud is a person who deceives others, claiming or being credited with accomplishments or qualities.

Dysfunction is not normal or is properly deviating from the norm of success. Behaviors always are regarded as bad when they are dysfunctional.

Your character will outweigh any lie told about you; remember that. Those who know you, know you. It's good to have people in your life who love you for you, people who see, encourage, and support the best in you. If someone wants to be slanderous, let them. If someone wants to believe their lies, let them. If someone wants to create and or get involved in drama, let them. Your life is a precious gift; your time is too valuable to be bothered with such silliness.

You cannot control what people think, speak, or do, but you can control how you respond. God reads our thoughts, hears our words, and sees our deeds, and remember, we will each one day stand before and give an account to Him (Romans 14:12). So don't let what someone else thinks, says, or does be your excuse for responding in a like manner.

Greed is an intense and selfish desire for scheming things, especially prosperity or fraud. Fraud is the wrongful or criminal deception intended to result in selfish financial or personal gains. A fraud is a person who deceives others, claiming or being credited with accomplishments or qualities.

More towers of righteous judgment will be served to publicly shame, humiliate, and humble the arrogant tyrants, bullies, criminals, and thieves spreading hatred, contempt, and false leadership, who use their power to purposely wreak havoc and chaos onto others.

Pride in oneself often leads to contempt for others. Restitution should be paid to all victims that were innocent. Greed is an intense and selfish desire for scheming things, especially prosperity or fraud.

Fraud is the wrongful or criminal deception intended to result in selfish financial or personal gains. A fraud is a person who deceives others, claiming or being credited with accomplishments or qualities.

Do not match your energy to someone who is gossiping all the time, bullying, and spreading vitriol and lies with bitter criticism. This person is not a leader.

They have an insensitivity to finding a solution or truth; instead, they focus their efforts on justifying their own lies, immoral behaviors, and actions. They laugh at another's downfall. This is not good behavior. There is no gray area; this behavior should never be tolerated.

Stand up to the bullying—this is not a good behavior. Period. No gray areas. Anyone who practices gossip and criticizing others is not considered capable of leadership. Spreading misinformation, lies, vitriol, bitter criticism, and hatred is hurtful and toxic behavior.

Why do people gossip? Gossipers justify their motives in various ways, but it comes down to low self-worth and personal integrity. They don't feel good about themselves, so they try to get attention by talking about others. This is typically someone they envy and are jealous of, or someone who has something the gossiper does not.

Gossipers don't realize they are hurting themselves more than their intended target. People who betray others' trust by spreading disrespectful or defamatory information about others should not be trusted. Spreading personal information or negative judgments is painful to others and reflects poorly on the gossiper.

After a while, I looked in the mirror and realized that after all betrayals, lies, backstabbing, harassment, threats, abuse, slander, gossip, bullying, hurtful behavior, trauma, scars, bruises, and all those trials, I really made it through. I did it. I survived that which was supposed to kill me. So I straightened my crown…and walked away like a boss still standing.

Nothing was ever hidden from the universe. You all messed with the wrong anointed chosen one. He is held in the highest honors in all realms.

Every action was seen, and righteous judgment was called. So now let's see if you can survive the same towers 100 times more than you gave out. Universal Karmic debt must be balanced.

Knowledge is youthful without a degree of faith. Where did you plant your seeds during your life? Replace "I should've known" with "now I know better." Forgive yourself, because self-shame is self-sabotage. Just because an answer seems ludicrous doesn't mean it's wrong.

What do you mean you don't like clowns? It's because you wear masks of illusion that you have the protection of secret societies. These clowns believe they are cloaked in masks of lies and are protected from their own hideous behaviors and actions, but they are not protected.

Remember, once something goes wrong in the circus, they send in the clown to distract the audience. Well, something has gone very wrong with the circus, and the clowns are everywhere.

You manifested this fear into your own life. I am everyone's nightmare and your worst dream come true; I'm everything you ever were afraid of. You manifested the same energy that you deserve.

Narcissists frequently use gaslighting tactics. Simply put, narcissists are cruel, manipulative, conniving, and convincing liars who consistently lie to cover up their indiscretions and manipulate to make everyone else think otherwise. They must know they are doing something wrong when they deny the truth with their fake personal charm and seduction and lure you in. That characterizes a narcissist. Anyway, you look at their actions and deny their participation in wrongdoing.

Look at their actions: they are duping you into believing that your perception of love with them is real, THEN they also dupe you into believing you are a horrible person, THEN they dupe you into believing you may have serious issues around your own mental health, and lastly, they dupe everyone around you into believing these horrendous lies to destroy you so they can move on to yet another unsuspecting target/victim. They start up the whole process

AGAIN and escape any exposure of what they are and what they have done!

EVERYTHING with them is a lie to support their needs and hide their agenda, and they constantly repeat this process with every person that they are in a relationship with. They even dupe friends into their lives to use as supporters or minions to support their facade of fake goodness.

You need to control your own whirlwinds of chaos and disaster that you created in your own life when you intentionally harmed others because you simply spoke your testimony and truth. Your truth holds power and cuts through the fodder of projection like a sword.

May you turn your sorrow into joy and turn their wickedness and lies into wealth. Instead, they punished you because you were honest and speaking the truth about their own hate crimes, cruelty, abuse, lies, toxicity and deceitful conduct to cause you harm and destruction. Does that make sense to victimize the victim? Your truth is your shield and armor.

They are throwing shade because they can't handle what they threw out to you. They know it's way too cold in their own dark shadows of shade to hide behind their shame. Throwing shade means a subtle sneering expression or contempt or disgust with someone for something. An enemy is a person who is actively opposed or hostile towards you.

Remember, your tyrant bullying actions, intentions, threats, thoughts, and words become your own reality. True leaders walk the walk. TThey don't talk about it, they be about it. They are not cowards skulking in darkness, throwing rocks, and hiding in their own shadows of shade.

Let the towers of truth and testimony bring down all the corruption, scam artists, magicians, practitioners, covenants cults, and false profits. Did you use your discernment to fight fake leadership? It's easy just follow the money; it always leads to their own greed and destruction.

Now let's talk about the facts, theory, and evidence that all of the below are not true leaders of the world.

A scam artist tricks or attempts to defraud a person or group after gaining their trust and confidence. They trick and exploit victims using a combination of the victims' nativity and greed.

A coven is a group or gathering of witches. They are definitely not divinely guided and definitely not of God.

A cult is a group requiring unwavering dedication to a set of outdated beliefs and practices which are considered deviant and outside the normal society. Cults are led by a charismatic and self-appointed leaders, not by God-appointed leadership. This self-appointed leader tightly controls its members.

Spiritual warfare is the Christian concept of fighting against paternal, pre-natural evil forces.

A false prophet is someone who speaks for another, but not for God. God does not own a bank account, and your soul and salvation cost nothing. Repentance is free and belongs to Him. Gollow the greed; it leads to the truth.

This was a test! The fallen will be judged together by the universe, which balances all unfairness. You were divinely guided, awakened, healed from the trauma, escaped, broke free of slander, drama, revenge plots, destruction, death, hatred, jealousy, envy, smirks, thieves, and arrogance. You broke free. All they cared about was their public image because you told the truth about their heinous games, strategic lies, and hideous actions.

You escaped years of lies and propaganda trying to block your destiny, journey, dreams, opportunities, and divine path and purpose. So they manipulated others to lie by payment of bribes and blackmailing through texts, emails, and letters in order to threaten them against spreading personal dirty laundry to exploit the skeletons in their own closets.

You escaped and broke free and campaigned with others to ruin your destiny and inherence set for you. If they were not going to have it, I wasn't going to have it either, so they purposely attacked my character with pitchforks. The universe, galactic justice, God all see the truth and will balance all in fairness. You must have faith that all will be rightfully balanced for you. Test your unblinded faith as you navigate through all the rocks that are in your path.

You cannot cheat your way into the divine kingdom. It's like stealing from the universe, God, and the spirit. They're trying to disrupt the disruption. You need to find what ignites your passions and soul. Stay grounded and true to yourself. Make a legacy that transcends throughout time.

Destiny is more about the journey than the destination. It's about self-growth and overcoming obstacles thrown on your path. Embrace the process and learn to celebrate the victories along the way. The true journey is about learning from the mistakes and the pursuit of your dreams, your self-belief, your confidence, and your limitless possibilities.

You hold the key to your own destiny and are the captain of your own journey. The universe will align to manifest your dreams. I believe in myself. Yes, others will become skeptical, but instead of seeking their approval, follow your heart. It speaks for your resilience and greatness within you. I trust in my journey to silence any naysayers. Whatever is yours is yours. Nothing can take away from your destiny. Divine timing was always at play. Trust that the universe will deliver. Set the stage for your own success through accountable leadership, active trust, and walking in faith to fulfill God's plan. Align your steps.

It doesn't matter what hardships you faced. None of us are throwaways because no one is ever beyond repair in God's eyes. Believe that He is the ultimate restorer of people, forgiveness, hearts, and lives. Restoration is the key to unlocking the kingdom and brings your own soul's transformation.

To manifest our own dreams, success, and happiness, we must have undeniable faith and believe our lives truly do matter to God. Hatred is poison to your soul, and no matter your beliefs, it will blindly lead you towards damnation, not salvation. It's your path, your choice, your journey, and your destiny.

Don't you think it's a bit of hypocrisy, blasphemy, and treason to believe the religious cross is a symbolic of spiritual Christian faith based on false leadership beliefs of the Roman Catholic religion? It's hypocrisy to believe that God would symbolize his son Jesus Christ's death by crucification and the cross? That is a man-made idol and is definitely not God-made.

Why in the world would God symbolize a cross, which is a Roman government ideology and is not aligned with God's law, which forbids idolization in the commandment to practice idolization? Why do we believe the Roman crucification of Jesus was his gift to the world?

The cross was not God's law it is Roman historical fact, but it is not to be used for the congregation to believe in this false profit, false guidance, and false religious beliefs. That is the true treason and is blatant treason and blasphemy to God.

Many of us are believe this fallacy, but it's false guidance. Remember, it was the Romans responsible for Jesus Christ's death by crucifying Jesus for his religious beliefs of Christianity. He was a prophet and healer who was christened and anointed by God himself as the true king of the kingdom.

It was Judas who betrayed Jesus and God based on man's Roman religion and the government's crucification laws. Jesus practiced God's law in the 10 commandments.

Idolization is the act of greatly admiring, revering, or adoring someone or something to the point of extreme devotion or excessive admiration, often seeing them as perfect or without flaws.

Crucification is a product of the Roman government and is not God's method of capital punishment. The condemned is tied or nailed to a large wooden cross, beam, or stake, and left to hang until eventual death.

The cross is recorded by man, not God. In 11th-century Old English, the word "cros" is used exclusively for the instrument of Christ's crucifixion, replacing the native Old English word "rood." The word's history is complicated; it appears to have entered English from Old Irish, possibly via Old Norse, and is ultimately from the Latin "crux" (or its accusative crucem and its genitive crucis), meaning "stake, cross."

A hypocrite is a person who indulges in hypocrisy: the story tells of respectable Ben who turns out to be a cheat and a hypocrite.

Intellectual property theft is against the 10 commandments, universal law, and civic law. It's like stealing Moses's commandments from his own home and claiming them as your original content.

It's blasphemy and treason to believe that any of your followers' words or work the past decade were actually written by you. You are all profiting off my ideas and gaining billions from my ideas. It's intellectual property theft, online stalking, hacking into personal property to steal and profit off your original content business ideas, solutions, and content that did not originate from you. You can never cheat your way into heaven.

None of these original posts, ideas, solutions were yours, and you were all tested to see if you would do the right thing. These ideas were given by God, but your own greed, pride, gluttony, arrogance, and profiteering proved you were not worthy of being trusted in a powerful leadership position.

All you cared about was getting paid and becoming the next up-and-coming influencer, but you didn't create any of this work. It was not yours.

Intellectual property theft is one someone steals an idea, creative expression, or invention from an individual or a company. IP theft can refer to someone stealing patents, copyrights, trademarks, or trade secrets. This includes names, logos, symbols, inventions, client lists, and more. Intellectual property theft cases are exceptionally common and require smart intellectual property management software in order to be avoided. Is intellectual property theft a crime?

Yes! Most intellectual property theft cases are considered federal cases and are therefore federal crimes. Companies or individuals that can identify who stole their IP and can bring them to court, and in some cases, serious penalties can be given to the criminals. These include fines, imprisonment, civil charges, suspension of licenses, and so on.

The History of Intellectual Property Theft

Theft is not a new phenomenon. The idea of intellectual property lates back to the 1700s (British Statute of Anne, 1710) when the idea of patents and copyrights were coming into place and the term "intellectual property" was born. Over time, the concept of IP theft has changed drastically, especially with the introduction of new technologies. From manufacturing processes and ideas in the industrial revolution to cybersecurity attacks and threats in the 21st century, IP theft has changed its face multiple times over the years.

You are the golden ticket, so assert your truth. Do not collapse under fears and doubts. All doors are open to you. You hold the key to change, happiness, and light. Restoring balance is very sacred to you.

Celebrate your justice. Listen to your higher power and purpose. You are a leader and the CEO of your own life. You do not have to prove anything to anyone, because it's not your burden and swords to prove or carry. You are set free.

Be strong and courageous and feel free with your peace, which is the key to light. My intentions are concise, clear, and deliberate. You have the power to change the world.

You have the power of the divine within you. You are freed from restraints. Even when the truth was in your face, you refused to stay in denial. My power of freedom is unconditional. It does not require outer circumstances to change or to feel your own freedom. Stay true to yourself. Live your authentic life, just ride the wave, be flexible, and go with the flow.

> I release all that brings me pain, anxiety, and fears.
> I release that blocks my growth.
> I release all that which is blocking love from my life
> I release all that which is toxic within me and around me.
> I release all that is not in alignment with my divinity.

Shine bright like a diamond and let your light irritate the demons. When God asks us to answer the call, we do it without hesitation.

The enemy retreats, trying to find ways to stop you. You are now operating at higher frequency level, which means your enemies no longer have the ranking to come against you.

You have graduated from the tests and lessons placed on your past and journey. All they can do is try to set traps of spiritual battlefield. Let God handle it—He sees the truth. The false accusations, cyber stalking, harassment, hatred, slandering, bullying, lies told, cheating, and plots to destroy you were an epic failure. The truth will prevail. Believe that the reign of terror is over and the cycle is closed. You learned the lessons.

Depravity is a moral corruption; wickedness; a tale of wickedness and depravity; or a wicked or morally corrupt act. Christian theology states that it is the innate corruption of human nature due to original sin.

There are consequences for the refusal of change. Deception is the illusion and thief and will not allow change to happen. Where did you plant your seeds to grow for the next generation? What legacy did you leave behind, or did you plant and nourish weeds? If you do not nourish your own soul and allow forgiveness for those who disappointed you, it will block your own blessings. To heal is to remain in balance. This leads you to your blessings.

Or did you choose to participate in jealous hate groups to dim and destroy my destiny? I am unbreakable and will never fall off my purpose. I should've come with a warning label! My only competition is the person in the mirror. I am my own unique brand. You should've picked the winning team. You cannot compete against someone who you don't compare to, and I am just getting started. I see your true colors.

You must become a strong leader. Wealth earned from wickedness will always be last. How can you expect any wealth or blessings if you participated in a targeted hater jealousy group against God, who gives the blessings? Let God handle them! You just need to have tunnel vision to remain on your anointed purpose to tell and share your truth, story, and testimony.

Remember, God can't bless mess. To be successful, you can't cheat your way into the kingdom, and you must do the work or the towers will continue to fall. Come up to a higher power; He called you to lead others by example.

Because you failed to use your moral compass, they will attack and bully the unprovoked because they are guilty for what they've done to you. So instead of trying to repair and fix the situation, they chose to go full throttle. When they realized they never really got away with anything, they told more lies on top of more lies to cover the deception and truth.

It's a sick obsession, and towers will continue to fall in their life. Choose to realize that you cannot copy my work, you can never compete with me, and you can never replicate me. You cannot fake it until you make it. Playing games with people's heart is exactly what happened to them. A moral compass is an individual's own personal set of personal beliefs and values regarding right and wrong. It serves as a guide to morally appropriate behavior. An unprovoked reaction is a display of aggression or emotion not caused by anything done or said.

The word of God is our moral compass, and it points us in the right direction. It seems that many of us has lost a moral compass to guide us as a society. True leaders do not compromise our conviction; they stand in the truth and speak with clarity to avoid confusion.

You cannot be upset at anyone but yourself for buying the snake oil, a substance with no real value which is sold as a remedy for all diseases. It is a product of little or no real worth or value.

It is promoted as the solution to a problem by the snake charmer, an entertainer who appears to make snakes move by playing music. Deception will always be exposed. The enemy will set traps for you, but use your intuition so you will not blindly walk into it. Use your discernment.

There are no random acts, encounters, or connections. Your North Star comes from within yourself. It's the moment you had a crashing realization that you were very wrong about someone or something and behaved horribly to someone and wronged them in some way.

It brought about a tower of shame and healing crisis, an enlightenment experience. This is actually good because it helped you map out the betrayals, but first remember to move the log from your own eyes without judgment.

The point in life is not winning at all costs; it's about applying the lessons. As a leader or captain of others, sometimes we have fears of change, but is it instant or training? To know this, you must understand the system and the limitations of the law. Is your process clear and concise? Then your decision as a leader will be absolute!

Spiritual stalking is a crime of universal laws and Karmic laws and must be balanced. I personally know people who engage with online psychics and intuitives to force story lines, and they go all the way to cause intimidation and "warning" towards individuals who dare to be their authentic self. They can spiritually spy on people to block opportunities and to control the outcome of their lives. They impersonate you to spy on your future. There is digital evidence.

These scare tactics, or I should say reverse psychology, will potentially break down those who are not mentally strong.

1. Suggesting video titles and specific words to be capitalized. Example: WARNING. You are advised to hold from making your next move.

2. Phychics/intuitives are given specific negative/hurtful words be used repeatedly throughout videos/content to "aim" target individuals.

Example: They thought you are stupid.

3. Impose as victim of circumstances and request stories to be shared publicly. These storylines are guilt trip "attacks" towards individuals who want to move forward and leave past behind. Those who engage with low vibration energies possibly may tamper with the intuitive downloads of others.

4. The masked storylines will eventually defame the other party.

We are determined to catch and punish those who try to take advantage of our citizens. This suspect thought they could use the trusted name of law enforcement to target innocent people. But we showed that we'll find them, no matter where they try to hide. There are always digital footprints of fraudulent money transfers and withdrawals into accounts. Greed always leads people into deception.

Don't worry what it may look like to others. Remember, Karmic and universal laws must be balanced. Those who participated in the plot to trigger a coup of shaming will be publicly humiliated for their deceitful attacks against you! You reap the same consequences as you deserve. Forgive those who didn't stand with you or tried to discourage you.

They will see your miracle come to pass in due time. Your job is to stay focused in your purpose and humble and let Him heal you, transform you, and fill you with His peace and joy. The enemy is getting more and more nervous every day watching you hold the line. He knows that if you outlast him, you will get ahold of your miracle and God's promises!

You are unstoppable to the world. You see what God sees. You hear what God is saying. Other people don't. They don't understand your assignment, and that's okay—it's not their assignment. You've got this!!

Integrity is value added. The world needs leadership that we can trust. People of integrity keep their word. They don't talk about it, they be about it. It doesn't matter what other people say or what their opinion is. All that matters is the person looking back in their own mirror.

The qualities of being honest and having strong moral principles and moral uprightness are the traits and qualities of leadership. The universe has a way of putting you in contact with people and things that are the same vibrational compatibility. It's okay to leave toxic people and behaviors behind. They chose not to elevate and to live in their own toxicity.

It's okay to leave people you have outgrown who no longer serve your higher purpose. The more you work on yourself and raise your own vibration, the more positive outcomes you'll experience. It's the laws of the universe.

Pay close attention to the projections of a narcissist's lies and accusations of their own dirty secrets hidden in their closets. They fear when you speak the truth about all their swords of lies, which they told to hide their truth of immoral betrayals.

They would rather take these devious, horrible betrayals to their graves and bury the truth without a confession. This is called projection, and the false bear witness in a court of law against me when they falsified documentation, defamed, slandered, gossiped, lied, and destroyed the character of an anointed chosen one. They slander the character of someone who tells nothing but the truth and use their own deceit to hide the 1000 swords of lies told about you without an ounce of proof.

For every lie told by the venomous snake who never made amends for their wrongdoings, there is Karma to balance and pay the same consequences. The truth is balanced, and the towers will destroy all of you who have participated. The truth spoken about every off-limits, dirty, secret relationship will be exposed publicly for the years of shameful lies.

Cowards sulk in their own hatred, jealousy, envy, false testimony, deceitful acts, and forbidden behaviors behind closed doors. The destruction is caused by you because of your sabotage, identity theft, plagiarism, stealing of intellectual property, stalking online, bullying, hatred, bigotry, bearing false witness, harassment, spreading gossip after the disclosure of revenge, and death threats when you told the truth.

You tried to bury the truth when you provided false witness and when you told others that you were in contact with me when, in fact, I never heard from you or received an apology for your wrongdoings. For over seven years, you made no contact and no amends for the toxic behavior towards me and slander that you were responsible for. You did not take accountability for any of your actions.

All of these horrible acts were yours that you projected onto me. None of it, not one word from you can be believed, and I can't understand how this happened without even asking the victim the truth and providing proof. Towers will fall to all who spat a venomous word, lied, gossiped, slanderd, defamed, and stole my identity and my inheritance. It is my destiny, not yours—it was never yours from the very beginning. You could never destiny swap with a divine power.

You chose the destruction of revenge against an innocent person and family that was held in the highest honors, an Annointed Starseed Chosen One. You chose to spy on my soul's purpose. You paid to stop God's plan and gave false testimony against a chosen one. You knew and still participated. There are no excuses. Don't you think that there will be severe retribution for spying by spiritual domination? Yes! it's true treason and blasphemy. You were never given permission, and there is a digital footprint in the Ether. There is no running from the Karma.

These actions cursed your life and bloodlines. You all knowingly worked together in a group to attack a chosen one. You thought it was a game. Well, I survived the secret society's years of bullying, torture, abuse, identity theft, theft of my intimidation, gaslighting, narcissistic behaviors, death threats, STDs, lies, fraud, forbidden rituals, poison, slander, and gossip. Everyone who participated is wishing you equal judgment.. as the abusers. You do not receive a hall pass. This was a choice you made.

Your word will continue to unravel because of the windstorm that you created in your own life. Anyone who was a spectator, who didn't throw the actual rocks, boulders, bricks, and stones, but watched the public stoning or the swords go into your back without helping you, in divine's eyes is deemed a coward! They laughed hysterically when you were stabbed by the knives and even chose to watch in divine's eyes. You will receive the very same Karmic consequences.

Again, where did you spend your valuable time? Were you planting a garden of abundant roses, or a garden of thorns? Never ever lower your vibrations to tempests, Jezebels, low-ranking statuses, and energy to meet theirs. It's okay; sometimes these tests did not help them learn the lessons in this lifetime. These are not your burdens to bear. You are not a vibrational match. They chose to break lifetimes of contracts with the divine.

You will receive a new vibrational match, a restart, do-over, because you were obedient to your calling, learned the barrage of unwarranted attacks, learned and applied these lessons by listening to your intuitive guidance, protected by the divine and universe. Following your divine contract and purpose without hesitation, or causing another lifetime of Karmic debt, is your legacy, your inheritance, your divine gift. When you have faith is when you receive the blessings you deserve. You can never cheat your way into your blessingsThat is a deceitful delusion.

So we're very clear, think about this: out of over 30,000 rejected opportunities and doors closed by my enemies, it only takes one chosen, divine door to open. Now, who is stronger? All you have to do is practice faith. I want to be on the winning team!

You can never ever curse a divinely chosen bloodline. What are you all smoking or high on to believe you are more powerful than God? This is definitely a God complex. Sit down and be humbled in your own humility for even thinking that was even possible. All doors are a test to see if you will blindly follow and open the right doors. Yes, we are here to learn, but no, I already opened that door and learned that lesson, and I never want to go back to that closed cycle again.

Please remember to remove the slander, gossip, lies, bullying, harassment, hatred, envy, jealousy, arrogance, ego, God complex, false leadership, venomous snakes, backstabbing, and corrupt secret societies from your own eyes without judgment. You can never handle their crimes of truth! This is the same exact energy you deserve, and is your Karmic balance thrown to you from the universe.

Let go, and let God handle your enemies, because absolutely not one second from the day you were born is forgotten or erased. It's a digital footprint of all your tests and how you applied the lessons. You can never swap destinies with the divine. That's a devil's illusion and lie.

Remember, he's a snake and a great liar, and he's here to test your faith. Therefore, you cannot cheat your way into elevation; you must do your own work. Do not lie; follow the commandments and universal laws. Do not heal a Judas snake and then get upset when he bites you again! It's their own Karma, not your burden to bear. These diseases and illnesses they have are from their own life of deceit. This is exactly what they chose. It's their projected life onto you and what they wanted you to believe: the false gossip, rumors, slander, stalking and bullying. Until you tell the truth, towers fall in your life.

When you give out love, grace, kindness, light and healing, you recieve the same energy as you deserve.

Liar, liar pants on fire. If only this really did happen, it would be more obvious to all when you lie, cheat, plagiarize, and commit fraud, identity theft, perjury, and stealing. This means there is no divine or universe connection. It's breaking several commandments, laws, and universal laws. It's blatant blasphemy and treason to believe that you're going to get away with this. You cannot cheat your way into the kingdom!

A person who tells lies is considered a liar! A liar is recorded in the Ethers as someone who is intentionally giving false statements, baring false witness, stealing, fraud, adultery, cheating, perjury, obstruction, identity theft, and plagiarism. They really believe you will not be prosecuted, punished, charrged, or convicted for aiding, lying, concealing, and committing conspiracy under oath. Period!

Drawing the line in the sand is really hard, especially when you know and finally realize that enough is enough! You are given a mustard seed of hope, love, and light; watch that seed grow into a plant, and then watch that plant grow into a garden. When you're God-tested and approved, who would be crazy enough to go against the divine power!

A true leader is legendary and is respected for their integrity in all realms, for their unwavering strength, compassion, honesty, loyalty, and knowledge, who always does the right thing no matter who is watching, because it matters.

Let go of jealousy, hatred, and envy, and let God handle the enemies! Have unblinded faith. No weapons formed against you will prosper when you have unblinded faith. Isolation is a great tower to build your own strength. You need to remember to love yourself, because that is the exact same energy that is going to come back to you, so it's a no-brainer right to love yourself. That is exactly what is going to come back to you.

Listen, not one person can provide salvation for your own soul except for God. It's your choices not anyone else's, not another man, not a church, not a pastor, not a religion, not an emporer dressed in a suit. Your soul's salvation is free by repentance. To manifest, you need to live enough. It's part of that game. You have to show God you love yourself, and if you do not show yourself love, how can you show genuine love to others? This is the secret to life's success.

Most people who think they matter won't be here the next day, the next week, and the next year, so it really doesn't matter what others think. Get up and show up every day. Everything is a return to sender, so why wouldn't you want to have that love, light, happiness, and joy return to you? It's the energy you deserve. Is this your legacy that you want to leave behind?

Everyone chooses their lessons. You do have free will, but you do not have the ability to avoid consequences! You can never be me, copy me, replace me, or have divine power over me; that is ridiculous to think you have power over divine power or authority above God's divine guided plans. You should know by now that everything that happened to you is exactly what you sent and was returned to you. It's Karma. Your job is to learn the lessons.

Who is the bigger fool? It's the ones who steal your powerful, inspirational motivational content, your divine downloaded messages and have the audacity to sell it and claim it was their own original content as powerful influencers. They are guilty of giving false testimonies and false incriminating evidence when they know it's a blatant and fraudulent lie.

Everything is recorded from the moment you were born into this world to ensure righteous judgment. You can't cheat your way into the kingdom of heaven. It breaks the Commandments, civil laws, and universal laws to steal, destroy, plagiarize, tell lies, slander, gossip, and abuse character. It's to ensure righteous judgment is served through Karma.

Fools will take your divine-given sword, stab you in the back, think you were ruined by their actions, and bet on your downfall, and every time you climbed up from catastrophic devastation, they plotted revenge. They spread hateful slander, lies, gossip, and character assassination to hide their own crimes of abuse. The fools are the people who blindly followed these tyrant bullies without questioning, evidence, or proof.

Tyrants are not to be feared, It's the people who act on the tyrants' words. These people are cowards and cannot be true world leaders. The wise will take all the swords and alchemize the hatred. They use these words given by God to cut their own cords and to free themselves from these fools!

Will an NDA contract save your divine soul? It depends on if you followed the divine's contract and signed transactions and the terms of agreements. You are protected from harm. If you choose to break a divine contract, the terms of the agreement are voided.

An NDA is known as a confidential agreement and is a legal contract between a between two parties that outlines confidential material or information that two parties wish to share with one another for certain purposes, but wish to restrict access to. No NDA contract will never cover your soul's salvation in the spiritual and universal laws. In fact, it's a violation, and that does not cover you. It definitely would be the divine or God's contract.

Remember, it's your soul, and the Devil is a great liar and will destroy you, no matter what it takes. The person or soul must pay lifetimes of Karmic death while he laughs in the corner because of the towers he made in your path. I am a living testimony of choices. I survived the boulders, rocks, bricks, and stones on my path and live to tell my story and testimony.

It seems several hundred people were involved in paid bribes while working at social media platforms and networks to copy, shadow band, harass, steal content, plagiarize, stalk, defraud, block, and spread hate.

When you paid employees to support your scandalous scheme, you all will have to face the same consequences of your actions. It's easy: just follow the money, and it will always lead to their greed.

RICO charges can be brought against you, and you can spend years in prison for aggravated harassment, lying, bearing false witness, hate crimes, stalking, defamation of character, and slander. There are literally hundreds of discriminating documents proving your company committed these crimes. Honestly, this type of behavior in a leadership position is not acceptable and should never be held in high honor, especially when you conduct or commit criminal acts. Did anyone ever seek justice for the victim?

Do not be the bigger fool who acts out; it's their manipulation to poke the bear! It's only a malicious and hurtful intention of manipulation to use others against you to gain control over your emotions. It's a test to see if they can lower and break down your high vibration to match them.

Control your temper, for anger only labels you the same fool! Get rid of bitterness, rage, anger, and brawling, along with every form of malice. Let go, God handle your enemies. It's the intention or desire to do evil and ill will. This is a test of your own inner strength and healing.

Stupidity is a them problem projecting onto you, especially when you highlight the weakness of their own immoral malicious wrongdoing, character offenses, leadership limitations, and failures. They lost their spiritual rankings, and now they are fake flexers. The higher vibration you remain in is the same energy you will receive, and you deserve the blessings.

A hierarchy of needs matrix was used against you to destroy your life. It's their secret society and is used for attacking any person to destroy them. This is exactly the same methodology and model used to attack me. When you attack someone's self-actualization, self-esteem, love and belonging, safety and security, and psychological needs, it can destroy a weaker-minded person, and they can succumb and become a victim of this tyranny.

It's a game they have contracted and used to create chaos in your life. They actually have companies contracted and paid to wreak havoc on each section of this hierarchy matrix. This is to cause undue mental distress. Because of my survival trauma training and endurance as a child, I survived these tactics.

I was able to break free from their attack patterns. I used my gifts of discernment and intuition to avoid their attacks. First, they attacked my self-actualization by attacking my morality, creativity, spontaneity, acceptance, experience, purpose, meaning, and any potential. Doesn't that sound familiar?

Secondly, they attack your self-esteem, confidence, achievement, respect of other's needs, and desire to be a respected and unique individual.

Thirdly, they attack your love and belonging, which means a coordinated effort to disrupt your friendships, family, intimacy, and sense of connections.

Fourthly, when they attack your safety and security, these secret societies will seek to attack your health, employment, opportunities, prosperity, family, and social stability.

Lastly, when they attack your psychological needs, they will block anything that is vital, like breathing, food, water, shelter, money, and sleep. I survived these heinous acts!

To exalt means to praise or hold someone or something in very high honor. If you failed your divine test, how can you believe the leader has the same power, ranking, and character status when they lost their credibility and protection? How can the fallen believe they are exalted to lead others with divinely guided messages?

Which one of you holds the true, authentic power of truth? There are only a select few chosen ones to be exalted, tested, and approved by God for all nations. Remember, there is only one way into to heaven, and that's through faith.

I fear the man who believes he has earned an exalted crown while knowing he lied and plagiarized his way through life. Here's the thing: only a few are exalted, so righteous judgment will be granted.

Be cautious when you falsify your testimony to speak untruths of uprightness, morality, and perjury.

How are you going to slide by God your judgment, bitterness, strife, animosity, resentment, faultfinding, slander, bullying, gossip, defamation, spitefulness, revenge, malice, and swords of betrayal in your cup? We need to remember that judgment is not ours and to love our enemies and pray for those who prosecute us. Here, you cannot fake it until you make it.

Sometimes Karma means you have to taste the same dish you served for others. Remember, the people who truly love and support you will outshine others' darkness be very proud of your healing as you continue to shine. You are not the last; you will be first. Believe in greatness and your growth.

Don't worry about insecurities of others. You absolutely do not need their validation. You started from the bottom, now you're here. Tou started from the bottom and now you're here. I have defeated my enemy. Don't let the squares in your circle; they will never fit.

Humble yourself, or God will do it for you! Focus on your purpose, faith, and trust, and believe in a little pixie dust! When you're cut off, it exposes their weakness, monstrous toxic behaviors, horrible traits, false divine prophecy, and fake reality and is their wake-up call!

Emotionally abusive partners are scammers. They scam others into believing you were the problem, too needy, too much, too weak, too sensitive. You didn't have enough money when they stole yours, and you were never going to be anything. Whenever you believe these lies and illusions, it makes their abusive tactics, tendencies, and untruths acceptable. The truth is that you deserved better. Do not give a narcissist time, attention, or oxygen.

Leaders share their wisdom and knowledge. When the doors open, run through them. It's time to manifest a new life. Know that your boundaries are not to be played with. I am electively social, not antisocial. We are busy blocking and blessing. It's easy when you tap into the high vibrational frequency of the universe. They didn't understand the assignment. That's okay; it's not their story or testimony to tell.

In this never-ending story, nothing is lost. Everything is transformed. It's never too late to create a different ending to your story. Never ending is having empathy for yourself to understand the ability to share the feelings of another. When I heal from grief and from any type of relationship or loss, I know I learned the lessons from loving wholeheartedly with my heart without their recyclable energy, or feelings.

It's unrequited love. This type of love is one-sided. It is unbalanced, unhealed love that will never be rewarded. The secret to balanced love is to love yourself and heal yourself, because no one's going to come rescue your soul or heart. It's your responsibility because it's the same energy you deserve returned. At the end of my journey, I can truly say I am a survivor, and that the finding, losing, forgiveness, forgetting, learning, remembering, leaving, and returning never stops.

The fact is, bad things happen to good people. The whole of life is about another chance while we are all alive. Until the very end, you have the ability to give and receive back the same energy and unrequited love you deserve. You can rewrite your own never-ending story! It's no one else's truth, story, testimony, or narrative to tell! The pages are blank and ready for you to create the best chapters of your life!

The problem with the world is that the highest intellectual people are full of doubts, while the stupid ones are full of confidence. Leadership requires us to practice integrity even when we believe no one is watching. Unfortunately, you will never gain another perspective if you continue to do the same actions over and over again with the same mindset.

It's like boxing: you spend hours practicing and knocking every opponent out because they never even came close to winning the championship against you. The delusional part is that they never had the endurance, inner strength, innovative talent, creative stamina, and status to win the title fight. It's their own delusional belief to compare themselves to an elite-level competitor. All they can really do is shadow box like a coward in their corner. They never had the sponsorship, clout, status, or spiritual ranking to earn their own, so like thieves, they collaborated with a group to steal your winnings like cowards hiding in their corner.

The towers of catastrophic destruction will continue to collapse all around you until you balance the Karmic debt. If you participated to mock God or steal for profit, you will receive the same wrath and lose your divine protection.

Every day, be grateful you are alive. You're never guaranteed another day! You are not broken! Nothing is wrong with you! Don't spend your valuable life and time trying to fix others! Believe in yourself and focus to move on!

Do not dwell on or lose your emotions, feel hurt, or brew on the people from your past who wronged you. The past is the past and means nothing in your future. Spend your energy on the things you can control, like loving yourself, forgiveness, positive mindset and attitude, inner strength, peace, and energy. It's the exact same energy you deserved. You have everything you need to heal. Don't lose yourself and self-esteem. Ground yourself every day.

Pray for gratitude for the things you cannot control or change. Leave any painful experiences behind. You have learned from these experiences and lessons, so send love, light, and gratitude. Do not let the past destroy your future blessings! Close and seal the doors of the past, and never open them again. Remember, you are the CEO of your own life! When God's your algorithm, trust him for guidance.

Silly rabbits, the sneaking around behind your back and betrayals are for kids! Being deceitful in your life has severe consequences and Karma. Trying to hurt others just hurts and curses yourself. It actually causes crashing towers in your own life. Just be extremely grateful, because God's rejection is actually for your own protection.

Remember, he sees everything, so if someone is removed out of your life suddenly, there is always a reason. You just need to hop along right through those open doors and give your past people an energetic goodbye hug. No one wants this person. It's delusional to think that the truth is the sneaking, conniving, and devious person! Yes, unity in a community has a whole different meeting now right!

This was a plot to take advantage of a power imbalance in order to hurt and exploit your kindness, love, healing, and vulnerability without any concern for your well-being. When fortune smiles on something as violent and ugly as revenge, it seems to be proof like no other that not only does God exist, He also sees every injustice and devious action. You're doing His will by loving yourself more. Let go and let God handle your enemies.

The same religious house exists today. Ignoring the fact that our identity as sheep comes from the character and person of the Shepherd, many of today's "Christians" have set out to explore dangerous ravines of self-fulfillment and high places of spiritual entitlement, unknowingly leaving themselves vulnerable, weak, and helpless to worldly predators. More towers of truth will fall. Teach your children that not everybody has good intentions. The world is a good place, but there are bad people in it. We may not be able to protect our children against everyone, but we can educate them to identify predators. We need a world rescue system.

These same preachers, popes, ministries, and practitioners spread hatred to hide their own lies and dishonest beliefs. These false religions are not faithful leaders of the new world, but emperors wearing masks, cloaks, and clothing. They have caused suffering for countless congregations and generations for their own selfish perverted sacrifices. They are victims of the scam artist and predators of innocent children. These perpetrators need to go prison for the protection of future victims. The church needs to be abolished and wealth allocated to the victims. They deserve psychiatric treatment for the sexual assault, abuse, and exploitation of innocent children.

The world needs a champion for change. If God does not own a bank account, where does all the money go? Follow the money; it always leads to their own gluttonous greed. Here's a novel idea surrounding greed in the world. All contributors, politicians, companies, corporations, governments, and agencies need to be audited. There should be one set of regulations for all nations to comply with. This includes worldwide rescue networks, shared global borders, standards, states, and resourses. There is no policy or political party above God.

Change is not on you, it's within you. Forgive them, love is all you need. Do not seek revenge. Try to see past their illusions and veils of destruction, because it will only destroy them. Remember, our thoughts and words are so powerful that what you speak becomes your own reality and truth. No weapon formed against you shall prosper. It's against spiritual laws, universal laws, and commandments to use forbidden weapons and rituals.

The consequences are that you lose your freedom, power, influence, rank, and integrity for intentionally targeting a divine. When using forbidden warfare tactics, it sounds an alarm because we are never alone. The choices were to fight for the enemy or get in alignment. Choosing the path of the enemy's attack will lead you to bite off more than you can chew, and you will fail miserably! It's a mission impossible.

Enemies act out in their own ego and will receive the same Karma. Embrace humility, or you will be humbled. You do not know the spiritual gangster warriors behind a heavily guarded divine. You cannot stand in front of someone else's price of treason. Justice will prevail and be balanced for participating in blasphemy against attacking humanity and the divinely protected.

Whatever tyrant, bully, haters, jealousy, or envy giant you are facing in your own life right now, all you need is unblinded faith in God, and that rock throne will defeat yours! David had to fight more giants after defeating Goliath, including his own family. Even after this victory, he remained vigilant. Remember, God has given us everything we need to defeat our own enemies and giants.

David prophesied this victory and spoke it into manifestation. He defeated this bully with faith and a single stone that sank into the enemy's forehead and sank a giant. Don't underestimate your own strength and power. You defeated the enemy because you trained for this battle since you were young. Stay ready, be ready.

Never give up, even when it means fighting for ten years, because one of those years could change your destiny and stars forever. You must do your own work, and there is no cheat code or shortcut in life. A bully tries everything to win at all costs by thieving and stealing someone else's lunch money every day to get ahead while pushing you out of the line.

It truly takes perseverance in doing something despite difficulty or delay in achieving success. Recognize that "the testing of your faith develops into perseverance." (James 1:3)

This is still a timeless masterpiece and relevant testament: "If you can't fly, then RUN. If you can't run, then WALK. If you can't walk, then CRAWL. But whatever you do, you have to Keep Moving Forward." (Martin Luther King, Jr.)

London Bridge is falling down, falling down, London Bridge is falling down. As you watch your own burning towers, you set a blaze to burn your own bridges, to open Pandora's Box, to eat the rotten, forbidden fruit!

The towers were caused from your own betrayals, secrets, lies, slander, cheating, deception, bearing false testimony, thievery, stolen money, stolen identity, daily stalking, mail tampering, character, assassination, stolen intellectual property, stolen property, and fraud you committed.

Do you ever feel you are forever stuck on a Karmic hamster wheel of life? Maybe it's because of your poly culture, or maybe it's the fact of spiritual attacks of hocus pocus you have sent towards me, or maybe it's the heinous crimes committed as a group of haters to hide your own reckless behaviors? Maybe it's because of some devious plots of revenge or because of your own recklessness.

You cannot stand in front of someone else's own treasonous actions. Karma must be balanced. Be grateful you were saved to tell your testimony and rescued off the hamster whell! You will be blessed for their own betrayals against a divine!

Reclaim your power back! If you don't like something, just take away its only energy and power by taking away your attention. Awakening is reclaiming and calling your power back. Listen, you were all tested! The inheritance never belonged to you. Lies travel fast, but the truth always prevails.

Hatred is a serious crime. Its unintended consequences spread fear in our community, and regardless of their intention, all crimes of hatred and bullying need held accountable. It has a direct impact on lives.

It doesn't matter if it's a scam, prank, or a credible threat; it should be handled as a viable threat and investigated. Maybe it's time for a new task force who uses AI to solve these types of increased threats. True leaders bring solutions to the problems. They do not talk about it, they be about it. Social media platforms can create an AI algorithm to capture these messages and make it safe for everyone.

This is my story about the corruption used against me and the hierarchy. These are exact words I posted over the last two weeks in a story. It's not their story. This is my survival story. This is proof that the secret society plagiarized my work. It's proof of their stalking, blocking, and stealing my creative intellectual property. Every word in this video is proof of their continued existence of criminal thieving, bullying, and charges against me. They think it's all a joke. If you look at my post about HMaslow's hierarchy and how they used it against me for the last 10 years, this is the exact same message. I posted my story, my survival, not theirs. Here is proof.

When your swords of truth cut through their binding lies, their masks of illusions fall off and expose all their hidden cloaks of deception and devious actions. This is caused by having a God complex, an unshakable belief characterized by consistently inflated ego and feelings of personal ability, privileged status, clout, or infallibility.

Remember, we cannot judge others. I refuse to allow our next generation to grow up with any fear complex towards nations, people, race, bigotry, color, groups, or religions. Let the power of God heal you from the pain, trauma, sorrow, and darkness covering the nation. No place is too dark or too difficult for the power and love of God!

Sometimes, we must experience darkness to appreciate the beautiful stars! Nothing grows in the shadows of darkness. The seeds of change were already planted and sown and will prosper. Maybe it's time for you all to spend time in Dirt Church or God's temple to appreciate his true majesty and to believe in a higher purpose, soul mission, and miracles again.

Yikes, this looks like when Moses warned against not follow the commandments, and Noah, Enoch's son, told everyone the flood was coming, and they laughed hysterically! Yes, it is true that confessions, apologies, and admitting the truth about your heinous, toxic, bullying behavior is good for your own healing. You can't trade your earned Karmic debt for divine blessings; that's another example of a devil in delusion. What are you all smoking or drinking to believe this was even possible? You deserve the very same treatment and will need to confess to lessen your soul's burden, but Karmic justice must be equally balanced.

If you participated in the debauchery, you receive the same Karmic storms. The elites are the most powerful divinely protected group and will always get up out of the mud when you go against God's planIf you accepted a bribe or money, you sealed your fate on your own path for you and your family. We all have choices and have free will, but we don't have control over the consequences.

This is a devilish delusion to believe you would ever be morally or ethically in alignment with divinity and exchange your life for the divine. You are actually motivating your enemies. Just be yourself. Telling your survival story is legendary. Be your own story. No matter what, everything will be exposed. If you knew about it, you will face the same Karmic, toxic storms. My journey was my self-discovery and success and was already written in the stars. When you watch that movie by Mark Wahlberg, *Affinity*, you get it you see the truth of the outcome of all these tests sent our way and particular situations beyond their control. Name a time in history when going against a divine purpose was successful?

Name a success in history or in the Bible of devious plots and plans to out maneuver fate that was correctly predicted? There is proof that every attempt ended up in fatality. Here are six example in the Bible: King David, Prophet Elijah's breakdown, John and Mark's desertion, Paul's awful history, Peter's denial of Christ, and Judas. Your story is still being written. The only way that failure can get the last word in your life is if you choose to let it. Listen. When we serve God, who is able to defeat enemies and is able to take our defeats and missteps, we bring glory to His name. You've been working with Him faithfully, or you've had a few stumbles along the way. Just have the undeniable faith that you will get back up again!

If you could say one thing to the bullies and haters who targeted and tested you knowing they were completely innocent, WHY?! No one likes to talk about their own elephants in the room, but instead of admitting you made really poor choices in your life, revenge is never the way! When you chose to heal from past trauma, lies, bullying, slander, hatred, manipulation, and sickness, you spread it to others, not me.

A divine takes time to heal themselves from past trauma in Divine Hermit mode for over 7 years. Celebate! This is a very painful process, but once you start healing from past trauma, your body begins to come out of fight or flight mode. In this unhealthy mode, your body will start to crave a lot of rest and silence. Your body finally starts to feel safe in peace and quiet. Calmness becomes your new self-love. You are not lazy; your body is just catching up and protecting your energy from all the years of chaos, fears, and turmoil.

While you're in healing mode, your enemies tried to knock you off your divine purpose. When you're strong and healed, the enemy cannot defer you off your North node. It's catching up on all the years that it didn't have the stillness you deserved. We learned from and appreciate those lessons and time to heal.

You are the vessel of your own success. No one, absolutely no one, can take it from you. When it is fate, the development of events by any person's control, determined by a supernatural power, the destined wheel of fortune or God's fate sets on someone's life and never can be deferred. The reason your whole life falling apart? You need to take a look at your own life. If you're not in alignment, this is a YOU problem. It is not someone else's to fix.

Fraud, stealing, lying, cheating, perjury, collusion, obstruction, and thieves violate God's commandments and will wreap God's wrath as a punishment. Thievery is when you have stolen messages, ideas, concepts, actions, and intellectual property obviously not created by you.

The divine messages were downloads from a chosen ascended master, not you. Changing a couple of words from someone else's work is treason and is considered intellectual property fraud.

If you've ever played the game Jenga, then you will understand this game of strategy. People really thought your life was a game.

They were trying to create faulty towers of chaos and hatred. They believed in control over your life. Every strategic move was calculated, and every building block was a well-thought-out vision of how they planned to execute a mission of misleading others.

As you were divinely guided to play fair with integrity, they played to strategically block God's next move. This game was played by people you cared for and trusted in your life. Every block of destruction was a wasted move. More lies built the tower. As the story builds, so does the suspense. Everyone knows that the towers of truth become weaker with each strategic move until the tower becomes too heavy. Under the tremendous lies, eventually the towers collapse in their own lives. This is Karma.

How they laughed as they pulled every strategic move to block your joy, happiness, love, and healing. People believed my compassion and kindness were weaknesses. I was the weak link in the organization, so they sought to destroy my foundation built by God. Every move He made was to help others build trust a stronger tower in their own lives of faith. Every step was ordered by Him and His grand design and purpose. If God is your architect, then towers become stronger and indestructible!

Why do we continue to trust false leadership when they strategically copy your divine messages, plagiarism, and modified guidelines? When you build with the true carpenter Jesus Christ and God, who is the architect of our lives, the enemies will blindly fail. Yes, we stumble and fall, but every time we get ourselves back up again. The dust settles and we can see the truth with clarity. Every attempt becomes easier as we build the towers of truth.

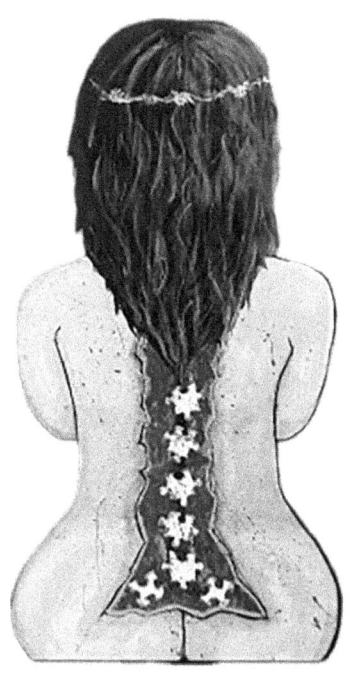

LET'S CONNECT

Melissa Foreman
Spiritual Transformational Life Leadership

LinkedIn
linkedin.com/in/melissa-foreman-bshcm
the-change-@ 4-66168835-be-

Website
www.nsls.org/

Email
frmnfmly@yahoo.com

Contact Number
209-681-2053

Zelle
WELLS FARGO
Manage payment profiles
Receive money with Zelle® O
Enroll your U.S. mobile numbers
and email address
Enrolled
209-681-2053
Email Account
frmnfmly@yahoo.com

www.ingramcontent.com/pod-product-compliance
Lightning Source LLC
Chambersburg PA
CBHW071708090426
42738CB00009B/1703